Olive Green English

B2

The authors of film dialogues and vocabulary lists: Wojciech Wojtasiak, Magdalena Warżała-Wojtasiak

The authors of grammar: Marta Borowiak-Dostatnia (A1-B1), Marcin Mortka (B2-C1)

The authors of interactive dialogues and vocabulary lists: Marta Borowiak-Dostatnia, Monika Glińska

Proofreading: Monika Glińska, Alicja Jankowiak, Natalia Wajda

Edited by: Alicja Jankowiak

Recordings: Graham Crawford, Joanna Haracz-Lewandowska, Jagoda Lembicz, Dale Taylor, Marianna Waters-Sobkowiak

Cover design: Marcin Stanisławski

Graphic design and composition: Wioletta Kowalska / Violet Design

Stock photos: © Fotolia.com

Publisher Chung Kyudo

Editors Cho Sangik, Hong Inpyo, Kim Taeyeon, Kwak Bitna

Designers Kim Nakyung, Yoon Hyunjoo, Im Miyoung

First Published December 2017
By Darakwon Bldg., 211, Munbal-ro, Paju-si, Gyeonggi-do 10881, Republic of Korea
Tel. 82-2-736-2031 (Ext. 550-553)

© Copyright SuperMemo World sp. z o.o., 2017
    SuperMemo is the registered trademark by SuperMemo World sp. z o.o.

© Copyright for the South Korean edition by Darakwon, 2017

All rights reserved. No part of this publication may be reproduced, stored in a retrieval system, or transmitted in any form or by any means, electronic, mechanical, photocopying, or otherwise, without the prior consent of the copyright owner. Refund after purchase is possible only according to the company regulations. Contact the above telephone number for any inquiries.
Consumer damages caused by loss, damage, etc. can be compensated according to the consumer dispute resolution standards announced by the Korea Fair Trade Commission.
An incorrectly collated book will be exchanged.

Price ₩12,000
ISBN: 978-89-277-0954-1 14740
       978-89-277-0950-3 14740 (set)

http://www.darakwon.co.kr
Main Book / Free MP3 Available Online
7 6 5 4 3 2 1   17 18 19 20 21

Table of contents

Introduction 4

Scene 1 (37): Martin and Beatrice 8
Future Continuous

Employees assessment • Talking about your working conditions • Expressing dissatisfaction • Suggesting possible improvements and solutions

Scene 2 (38): Picnic in the park 16
Extreme adjectives • -ish ending for adjectives • Articles: the, zero article

Discussing the life and work of famous people from the past - Shakespeare • Presenting facts, conjectures and interpretations

Scene 3 (39): Confronting the parents 24
Future Perfect • Future Perfect Continuous

At the post office • Sending letters and parcels • Comparing postal charges

Scene 4 (40): News of the wedding 32
Past Perfect Continuous

Paranormal phenomena • Talking about the UFOs, zombies, ghosts etc.

Scene 5 (41): Scuffle on the road 40
Past modal verbs

Sharing your life events and experiences • Talking about hard times • Expressing grief and sympathy

Scene 6 (42): Planning revenge 48
wish • if only • it's high/about time • I'd rather

Talking about difficult life experiences (like divorce or death) • Necessary formalities • Expressing outrage, sense of injustice, sympathy • Offering condolences

Scene 7 (43): Wake-up call in the park 56
Verbs with infinitive and gerund • As if/though

Contacting the property administrator • Reporting a problem • Arranging a meeting with a technician

Scene 8 (44): Request for help 64
Third Conditional • Emphasis with do

Talking about your situation and changes at work • Considering different paths of career and personal development • Interpersonal conflicts in the workplace

Scene 9 (45): Meeting Willis 72
Word building: suffixes, prefixes • Compound nouns

Negotiations between companies • Negotiating with the trade unions • Seeking the compromise

Scene 10 (46): Confrontation 80
Defining relative clauses • Non-defining relative clauses • get/have something done

E-payment methods and uses • Ideas for an online business

Scene 11 (47): Shots are fired 88
Passive voice with modal verbs • it is thought/known/believed that

Reading manuals for electronic devices • Writing a blog • Tips on how to use online platforms

Scene 12 (48): Murray flees 96
Advanced reported speech

Business presentations • Presenting results, discussing charts and graphs • Presenting the action plan for the future

Translation 104

Introduction

Olive Green is an innovative course for those who want to learn English from the beginning in a way that is both modern and efficient. It is the perfect combination of fun and effective learning of the highest order.

The **Olive Green** multimedia course is based on an **interactive action film**, where you can decide what course the plot will take, as well as play some arcade-type and language games. The course is divided into 12 film scenes for each language skill level.

What is the best way to learn with the Olive Green course?

To begin with, watch the right **film scene** in the multimedia course. We encourage you to watch it several times, so that you can gradually get used to the natural pronunciation you hear and make decisions during interactions. The **subtitles** (available in English and many other languages) will help you understand the content of the dialogue. If you are learning English from scratch, first watch each scene with subtitles in your own language (if available), then with English subtitles, and finally without subtitles. Next, read the **text of the film dialogue** in the book. Then listen to the MP3 recordings of the dialogue, and lastly try to read the text aloud.

Each scene in the book is accompanied by a **list of new words and expressions**. Read them and find them in the dialogue to see how they are used in context, and then listen to the recording of the list.

In the next step, please read the **grammar explanations** describing the most important topics introduced in each film dialogue. You will find many examples of typical applications of all the new structures in these sections.

The multimedia course also includes **interactive dialogues** to let you practice in a variety of communication situations and develop the skills necessary for a conversation in English. Additionally, selected variants of these dialogues have been included in the book, together with the lists of new words and phrases that will help you expand your vocabulary for each topic.

Last but not least, read the **cultural commentary** that will introduce you to some interesting aspects of the culture of the English-speaking countries. The language of the commentaries is simple, but if you are just starting your adventure with English, it may be hard to understand. In that case, please remember that it is always better to try to analyze and understand the general meaning of any English text on your own first – especially if you have been working with the course for some time. Consulting a dictionary for definitions or equivalents of the words that may be new to you should generally be your "second best" option.

To those who wish to continue learning English with **Olive Green**, we recommend the rest part of the course at the other levels.

Enjoy your learning!
The SuperMemo World team
& Darakwon Olive Green team

Olive Green

level B2

Scene 1 (37)   Film dialogue and vocabulary

Read the dialogue between Martin (M) and his uncle (U). Check the list of words and phrases below.

Martin, you wouldn't know where I put the god damn invoices for Brian Davidson, would you?

Be amazed, Uncle!

M: In this very drawer you'll find all the invoices from the last 6 months – sorted in chronological order.

U: What did I tell you? You'll be running this place in no time! ... Now, there's one more place I want you to stop by before lunch. You'll love it there!

Vocabulary			
invoice	송장	sort	분류하다
amazed	놀란	in chronological order	시간순으로
uncle	삼촌	lunch	점심
drawer	서랍		

level **B2**

Read the dialogue between Martin (M) and Beatrice (B). Check the list of words and phrases below.

M: They'll look astonishing on the dining table of the rich old farts from the manor!

B: The rich old farts from the manor couldn't care less about flowers. They say they look pretentious.

M: So, why did they hire you if they don't like flowers?

B: I do it for fun. This place is excruciatingly boring. I'm Beatrice Campbell. The daughter of the stinking rich old farts from the Manor.

Vocabulary			
astonishing	놀라운, 눈부신	hire	고용하다
dining table	식탁	excruciatingly	극심하게
old fart	노인네	daughter	딸
pretentious	가식적인, 겉치레뿐인	stinking rich	엄청나게 돈이 많은

What should Martin do?

ask Beatrice out

leave

M: I'm Martin. ... Look, I can't leave you being so bored. It'd be inhumane. How about you and I go for a drive?

B: Drive?

bored	지루한
inhumane	비인간적인

B: Look, I might need a delivery service very soon! Can I call you or are you busy these days?

delivery service	배달 서비스
busy	바쁜

Grammar explanations

미래진행 Future Continuous

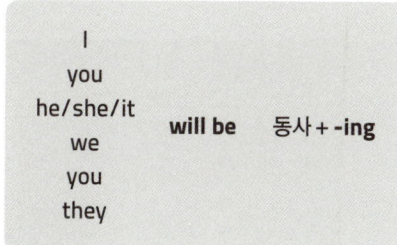

Don't call me at four o'clock. I **will be trying** to organise the invoices. 4시 정각에는 저한테 전화하지 마세요. 저는 청구서를 작성하고 있을 거예요.

My mother will be absent next weekend. She **will be meeting** her posh friends at the Ritz. 저희 어머니께서는 다음 주에 집에 계시지 않을 거예요. 리츠에서 부유한 친구들을 만나고 계실 거예요.

This time next week we **will be looking** for a new employee to hire. 다음 주 이맘때쯤 저희는 새로 채용할 직원을 찾고 있을 거예요.

미래진행의 의문문과 부정문 Questions and negatives in Future Continuous

미래진행형 문장의 의문문/부정문 변환은 단순미래형 문장의 의문문/부정문 변환의 규칙을 따른다.

I **will be having** a meeting at 2 o'clock. → **Will** I **be having** a meeting at 2 o'clock? 저는 2시에 회의를 하고 있을 거예요. → 제가 2시에 회의를 하고 있을까요?

My aunt **will be working** in her study at this time tomorrow. → When **will** my aunt **be working** in her study? 저희 고모는 내일 이 시간쯤 공부를 하고 있을 거예요. → 고모가 언제 공부를 하고 있을까요?

The hired man **will be following** his target in the streets of London tomorrow from 8 to 11 p.m. → The hired man **won't be following** his target in the streets of London tomorrow from 8 to 11 p.m. 고용된 사람은 내일 런던 거리에서 오후 8시부터 11시까지 자신의 타깃을 미행하고 있을 거예요. → 고용된 사람은 내일 런던 거리에서 오후 8시부터 11시까지 자신의 타깃을 미행하고 있지 않을 거예요.

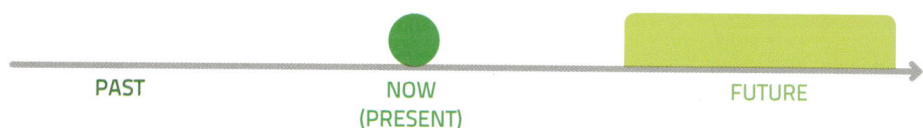

1. 미래진행형은 미래의 어느 시점에 진행되고 있을 예정된 활동이나 계획을 나타낸다.

   Next weekend I **will be admiring** the delights of London.
   다음 주말에 저는 런던의 재미를 만끽하고 있을 거예요.

   Tomorrow at three o'clock I **will be hiring** new employees for our Birmingham branch.
   내일 3시에 저는 버밍엄 지사의 신입 사원을 채용하고 있을 거예요.

2. 미래진행형은 미래의 어느 시점에 확정되어 진행될 일을 나타낸다.

   Olive **will be running** away until she finds a safe place for herself.
   Olive는 본인에게 안전한 장소를 찾기 전까지 도망 다닐 거예요.

3. 미래진행형은 미래에 대한 정중한 질문을 할 때 사용된다.

   Will you **be having** coffee with us after the concert?
   콘서트가 끝난 후에 우리와 커피를 마시지 않을래요?

Communication situations

Read the following dialogues between a boss and his employee during his performance review.

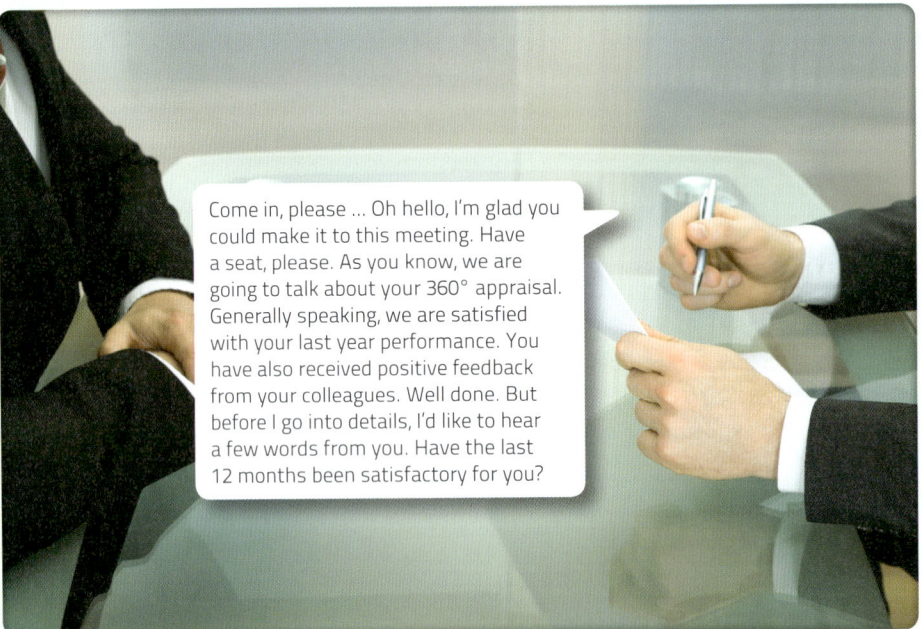

Come in, please ... Oh hello, I'm glad you could make it to this meeting. Have a seat, please. As you know, we are going to talk about your 360° appraisal. Generally speaking, we are satisfied with your last year performance. You have also received positive feedback from your colleagues. Well done. But before I go into details, I'd like to hear a few words from you. Have the last 12 months been satisfactory for you?

Dialogue 1

Employee: Yes, I have been satisfied with my performance. Nevertheless, there are a few things I'd like to talk about.

Boss: Namely?

Employee: I'd like a reduction in my workload.

Boss: I see. But you were informed about the scope of your work when you took the job.

Employee: Not exactly.

Boss: How come?

Employee: We started more projects than planned. And now I'm snowed under.

Boss: Oh, I see. Well, you should take it as a challenge.

Employee: This kind of challenge kills my motivation.

Boss: Well, I'm sorry to hear that.

performance 성과 I nevertheless 그럼에도 불구하고 I namely 즉, 다시 말해 I inform 알리다 I workload 업무량 I snowed under (많은 일에) 파묻혀 있는

Dialogue 2

Employee: I'm glad I met my target. But quite a few things were less than perfect.
Boss: Namely?
Employee: Your incentive programme simply doesn't work.
Boss: What do you mean?
Employee: Well, there is no holiday pay, no sick pay, and no pension scheme.
Boss: Not quite. You get all of them as you take a higher position in the company. But that takes time and involves hard work and commitment.
Employee: And what do you mean by commitment? Answering the phone at midnight?
Boss: That's not the main determinant, you know.

meet target 목표를 달성하다 I incentive programme 인센티브(장려금) 프로그램 I holiday pay 휴일 근무 수당 I sick pay 병가 수당
pension scheme 연금 제도 I commitment 헌신 I answer the phone 전화를 받다 I main determinant 결정적인 요인

Dialogue 3

Employee: Yes, they have. Mainly due to my excellent results.
Boss: Indeed. Your results have been impressive.
Employee: I'm glad you appreciate that.
Boss: You're a valuable member of our team. Nevertheless, there is always some room for improvement.
Employee: Well, in terms of my performance, time is money.
Boss: I agree. Go on, please.
Employee: Commuting takes too much of my time.
Boss: What solution do you suggest?
Employee: I'd like to work from home twice a week.
Boss: Oh, I'm afraid it's out of the question for the position you hold.

result 결과 I room for improvement 개선의 여지 I Time is money. 시간이 돈이다. I commute 통근하다, 통학하다 I twice 두 번 I
out of the question 논의가 불가능한 I hold the position 지위를 차지하다

level B2 Scene 1 (37)

Vocabulary plus

assembly point 집회장

bear in mind 명심하다

case of emergency 위급한 상황

chained to one's desk (일 때문에) 책상에 매여 있는

clash 충돌

cramped 비좁은

daylight 햇빛, 일광

define 정의하다, 한정하다

do one's duty 본분을 다하다

efficiency 효율, 효율성

emergency exit 비상구

evacuation route 대피 경로

exaggerate 과장하다

facility 시설

fire alarm 화재경보기

fire extinguisher 소화기

fire hazard 화재 위험

first-aid kit 비상약품 상자

get back to ~로 돌아오다

H&S (Health and Safety) 건강과 안전

harmful 해로운

in a way 어느 정도, 어떤 면에서는

in comparison to ~와 비교할 때

in deep trouble 심각한 곤경에 처한

independently 독립하여, 자주적으로

make dry 말리다

not to mention ~은 물론이고, 말할 것도 없이

observe 준수하다, 지키다

on duty 근무 중인

pace 속도, 보폭

projector 영사기

put into practice 실행에 옮기다

read between the lines 숨겨진 의미를 파악하다

red tape 형식적인 절차, 불필요한 요식

regulations 규정

relocating 이전

reorganize 재조직하다

shortcoming 결점, 단점

sign 표지, 표식

stimulating 고무적인, 자극이 되는

supervisor 감독관

take as ~로 간주하다

task-oriented 업무 중심의

temporary 일시적인

unhealthy 건강하지 못한

wish list 소원 목록

with someone breathing down your neck ~에게 감시를 당하는

work schedule 근무 스케줄

Cultural tips

Did you know that …?

The English garden is a style of landscape garden which was developed in England in the early 18th century, and spread across Europe, replacing the more formal, symmetrical French garden. The English garden usually includes a lake, lawns, groves of trees, classical temples, Gothic ruins, bridges etc.

Scene 2 (38) Film dialogue and vocabulary

Read the dialogue between Beatrice (B) and Martin (M). Check the list of words and phrases below.

Superb vintage! Has an exquisite taste! And a perfect addition to seafood and quality cheeses.

Good because I happen to have some cheese crackers.

B: What about your parents? Can't they chip in to pay for your studies?

M: No! Whatever money they lay their hands on they just waste on booze! Pretty messed-up people if you ask me.

B: They can't be worse than mine! My dad – the head of the local fox hunting association and my mum … Her sole concern is keeping her face wrinkle-free so that she looks stunning when she meets her friends at the Ritz in London.

M: They seem mental all right! But they did produce an okay-ish daughter. Acceptably pretty, not too stupid, slightly weird, though.

B: Slightly weird?

M: Yeah, but I like your weirdness.

Vocabulary

superb	최고의	fox hunting	여우 사냥
vintage	(고급) 포도주	association	협회
exquisite	더없이 훌륭한	sole	유일한
taste	맛, 풍미	concern	관심사
addition	추가	wrinkle-free	주름 없는
seafood	해산물	stunning	놀라운, 굉장히 아름다운
quality	질, 우수함	mental	제정신이 아닌
cracker	크래커	produce	낳다
parents	부모님	okay-ish	적당히 괜찮은
chip in	(돈을) 보태다	acceptably	만족할 수 있게
studies	학업	slightly	약간
lay one's hands on	~에 손을 대다	weird	이상한
booze	술	weirdness	이상함
messed up	엉망인		

level **B2**

What should Martin do?

insist

apologize

M: There's nothing to be afraid of!

B: One thing you should bear in mind if you want to see me again: never push it!

M: I won't! Ever! But ... what if next time the conditions are more favourable?

M: Sorry. That was way out of line!

B: It wasn't that bad, but it's not how these things are done in Campbell Manor.

M: How are these things done in Campbell Manor?

B: Stick around long enough and you may find out!

Vocabulary

bear	지니다
push	몰아붙이다
ever	언제든, 한번도
conditions	상황
favourable	호의적인

stick around	머무르다

Grammar explanations

극단 형용사 Extreme adjectives

terrible, freezing, terrifying 등과 같은 형용사는 이미 *very*의 의미를 내포하고 있다. 그러므로 *very*와 함께 쓰이지 않는다.

terrible = very bad
terrifying = very scary
packed = very crowded
deafening = very loud
starving = very hungry
exhausted = very tired

freezing = very cold
hideous = very ugly
hilarious = very funny
tiny = very small
furious = very angry

*-ish*로 끝나는 형용사 Adjectives with the *-ish* ending

어미 *-ish*는 *rather / slightly / a bit / somewhat*의 의미를 내포하고 있으므로 *-ish*를 어미로 둔 형용사는 상대적으로 의미의 강도가 약하다.

longish = slightly long
youngish = rather young
grayish = a bit gray
greenish = a bit green
longish = rather long

bluish = a bit blue
darkish = rather dark
hottish = slightly hot
fattish = rather fat

관사 Articles

*the*는 아래와 같은 경우에 쓰인다.

- rivers (**the Nile, the Vistula**)
- seas (**the North Sea, the Black Sea**)
- mountain ranges (**the Himalayas, the Alps**)
- island groups (**the Falklands, the Antilles**)
- hotels, museums and theatres (**the Ritz, the Hilton, the Globe Theatre, the Olivier**)
- deserts (**the Sahara, the Gobi**)

*the*는 아래와 같은 경우에 쓰이지 않는다.

- continents (**Africa, Asia**)
- lakes (**Michigan, Balaton**)
- mountains (**Ben Nevis, Mont Blanc**)
- cities and towns (**Moscow, New York, Belfast**)
- streets and shops (**Baker Street, Selfridges**)

대부분의 국가는 *the*와 함께 쓰이지 않는다.
in Japan, in Germany, in Poland etc.
하지만 예외도 있다.
**in the United Kingdom, in the USA, in the Czech Republic, in the Philippines,
in the Netherlands**

*the*가 생략되는 경우:
직위와 이름이 함께 쓰일 때, *the*는 생략된다.
the president of the country – President Chirac
Tomorrow **the president of the country** will give a speech.   내일 그 나라의 대통령이 연설을 할 것입니다.
Tomorrow **President Chirac** will give a speech.   내일 시라크 대통령이 연설을 할 것입니다.

the king of England – King James II
The king of England was traditionally crowned at Westminster.
영국 왕은 전통적으로 웨스트민스터에서 즉위를 했습니다.
King James II was the last Catholic king of England.
제임스 2세는 마지막으로 가톨릭교를 믿었던 영국 왕이었습니다.

the admiral of the fleet – Admiral Nelson
The admiral of the fleet ordered to set sails at dawn.   그 함대의 제독은 새벽 출정을 명했습니다.
Admiral Nelson ordered to set sails at dawn.   넬슨 제독은 새벽 출정을 명했습니다.

*the*가 생략되는 그밖의 경우:
일반적인 사물
Dogs are friendly.   개는 다정합니다.
Coffee is good for us.   커피는 우리 몸에 좋습니다.

게임이나 스포츠
Let's play **football**!   축구를 합시다!
Anyone care for a quick game of **tennis**?   테니스 한 게임 할 사람 있나요?

질병
My friend has contracted **malaria**.   제 친구는 말라리아에 감염되었습니다.

학교 과목과 학문
I was never good at **maths**, yet I am studying **economics**.
저는 결코 수학을 잘하지는 않지만 경제학을 공부하고 있습니다.

식사
What's for **breakfast**?   아침 식사는 무엇인가요?

요일과 월
Let's meet on **Tuesday**.   화요일에 만납시다.
Is it **January**?   1월인가요?

Communication situations

Read the following dialogues between a certain professor and the host of the lecture on the life and work of Shakespeare.

Professor Malvolio, thank you for this fascinating lecture about the life of Shakespeare. Some of your findings certainly seem surprising. Would you be willing to stay a moment longer to answer some questions we've collected from the audience?

Dialogue 1

Professor: Of course, I'd be happy to answer any questions.

Host: One question always sparks particular controversy. Did Shakespeare write all his plays alone?

Professor: I dare say he was not the only author of his alleged works.

Host: So, was it a whole team of writers or just one co-author?

Professor: I'd say it varied from play to play.

Host: How can you be so sure?

Professor: He vividly describes experiences that couldn't have been his. Like travelling around Europe, for example.

Host: What kind of argument is that? Would you also question Tolkien's authorship of The Lord of the Rings because he'd never been to Middle Earth? Anyway …

---

lecture 강의 | spark particular controversy 논란을 일으키다 | dare say 아마 ~일 것이다 | alleged 주장된 | writer 작가 | vividly 생생하게 | experience 경험 | question 의심하다 | authorship 저자

Dialogue 2

Professor: I will do my best to fill you in.

Host: All right. The first comment concerns Shakespeare's private life.

Professor: No wonder. This part always attracts a lot of attention.

Host: What about his sexual preferences? We know that he was married but was it just a cover?

Professor: The issue is even more complicated than that.

Host: What do you mean, Professor?

Professor: Some traces found in his literary output seem to suggest that Shakespeare was actually a lady.

Host: But isn't that a misinterpretation - or even an over-interpretation - of his writings?

Professor: There is such danger, of course. But we are talking about prominent researchers here.

Host: I see. Let us talk about the sonnets now. Their authorship is also highly controversial in the eyes of many.

private 사적인 l **sexual preferences** 성적 취향 l **controversial** 논란이 많은 l **literary output** 문학 작품 l **misinterpretation** 오역 l **over-interpretation** 확대 해석 l **prominent researcher** 저명한 연구가 l **in the eyes of** ~의 눈으로 볼 때

Dialogue 3

Professor: Well, we know that he was married and had children.

Host: Of course, but his sexuality has been questioned many times, has it not?

Professor: His sexuality is just the tip of the iceberg.

Host: What do you mean, Professor?

Professor: According to one theory, "Shakespeare" was just another identity of the playwright and poet Christopher Marlowe.

Host: Wait, what? Are you saying that some researchers question Shakespeare's very existence? Dear me ...

sexuality 성적 취향 l **according to** ~에 따르면 l **identity** 신분; 정체성 l **playwright** 극작가 l **existence** 존재

Vocabulary plus

achieve 성취하다
affair 정사, 불륜
argument in favour 찬성하는 주장
attraction 매력
bisexual 양성애의, 양성애자
collaborate 협력하다
conduct 수행하다
creator 창조자
critic 비평가
cultural heritage 문화 유산
Dear me! 저런!
deliberately 고의로
diversification 다양성
find something hard to believe 믿을 수 없는 것을 발견하다
findings (조사) 결과들
further evidence 추가 증거
heterosexual 이성애자
in the light of research 연구를 참고하여
level of education 학력

mainstream 주류
means of poetic expression 시적 표현의 수단
metaphor 은유
occasional 때때로의
pen name 필명
period 시기
phrase 구절
privileged background 특권층 출신
prodigy 영재
put on display 전시하다
puzzling 헷갈리게 하는
resemble ~와 닮다
ruler 통치자
strong statement 강한 표현
tackle (문제 등을) 다루다
tedious 지루한
vary 다르다
weak 약한
well-educated 교양 있는

Cultural tips

Did you know that ...?

Fox hunting is an activity involving a group of people on horseback, chasing a fox across open countryside with a pack of foxhounds, often, but not always, ending with the hounds killing the fox.

Scene 3 (39) Film dialogue and vocabulary

Read the dialogue between Beatrice (B) and her father (F) and mother (M). Check the list of words and phrases below.

M: Bright enough to seduce and brainwash a 17-year-old girl?

F: What your mother is trying to say is that we've got reasons to believe your boyfriend's got a different agenda than you think!

B: What are you talking about?

F: Look, as soon as you two start living together, God knows where, he'll get you pregnant. By winter of next year you'll have delivered an heir to all our financial assets. As the father, he'll be entitled to a big share of this money!

B: Where's all this poison coming from?

M: These things happen, darling. Frauds, thieves and other scum! Our class of people is under constant threat!

F: Beatrice, you're not of legal age! So we don't permit your moving out or even seeing that man. In a couple of months ... suit yourself!

B: Is that it?

F: No, it's not! You and your mother are about to go away for some time.

M: Yes! Before you abandon us, I want to have you for myself for a few months.

B: So that by the time I'm 18 you'll have been trying to change my mind about Martin for half a year?

F: What is half a year for people so committed to their relationship?

level B2

Vocabulary	move out	이사를 나가다		financial	재정적인
	live	살다, 거주하다		assets	재산
	truck driver	트럭 운전사		entitled	자격이 있는
	aspiration	야망		poison	독, 독이 되는 사상이나 감정
	high	높은		scum	쓰레기 같은 인간
	bright	똑똑한		class	계급
	seduce	유혹하다		constant	끊임없는
	brainwash	세뇌시키다		be under threat	협박 받다
	boyfriend	남자 친구		permit	허락하다
	agenda	의제		suit oneself	마음대로 하다
	be pregnant	임신하다		abandon	버리다
	winter	겨울		change one's mind	마음을 돌리다
	deliver	출산하다		committed (to)	~에 전념하는
	heir	상속자			

What should Beatrice do?

B2-03-02
object

B: I'm not going! You won't separate me from Martin!

F: Oh no? Let's think: coercing an under-age girl to drink and he's been here, in the Manor, without us knowing, hasn't he? Perhaps some property was stolen on the occasion. We really should look into this, shouldn't we?

B: All right! ... But once I'm back, that'll be the last time you see me!

agree
B2-03-03

Vocabulary	separate	떼어놓다
	coerce	강요하다
	underage	미성년의
	property	재산, 소유물
	on the occasion	즈음하여, 그때

B: Yeah, why not? But these six months will not change how I feel about him!

Grammar explanations

미래완료 Future Perfect

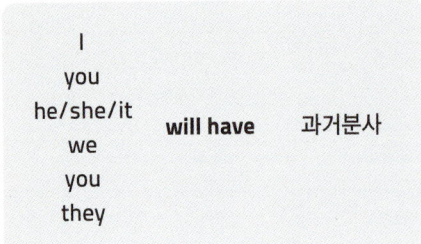

Olive **will have** stolen the painting by the end of the week.
주말까지 Olive가 그림을 훔칠 것입니다.

미래완료형은 미래의 어느 시점에 종료되는 일을 나타낸다.

I **will have** discovered all Olive's secrets by the end of the film.
저는 영화가 끝날 때까지 Olive의 비밀을 모두 알게 될 것입니다.

I **will** also **have** learnt tons of new words in less than two months.
저는 또한 두 달 이내에 많은 양의 새로운 단어들을 익힐 것입니다.

미래완료형은 기한과 시점을 나타내는 'by + 시간 표현'과 함께 쓰인다.

I have just started learning Norwegian. I **will have** learnt the basics by the end of the year.
저는 노르웨이어 공부를 시작했습니다. 올해 말까지 초급 과정을 익힐 것입니다.

미래완료형은 기간을 나타내는 'in + 시간 표현'과 함께 쓰인다.

I **will have** learnt the basics in six months / in six months' time.
저는 6개월 내에 초급 과정을 익힐 것입니다.

By Tuesday I **will have** watched all the episodes of Olive Green.
화요일까지 저는 Olive Green의 모든 에피소드를 시청할 것입니다.

In two weeks' time I **will have** watched all the episodes of Olive Green.
2주 내로 저는 Olive Green의 모든 에피소드를 시청할 것입니다.

미래완료: 의문문과 부정문 Future Perfect: questions and negatives

My father **will have learnt** how to scuba dive by the end of his holidays.
→ Who **will have learnt** how to scuba dive by the end of the holidays?
누가 휴가가 끝날 때까지 스쿠버다이빙을 배우실 건가요? → 저희 아버지께서는 휴가가 끝날 때까지 스쿠버다이빙을 배우실 것입니다.

What **will** my father **have learnt** by the end of the holidays?
저희 아버지께서는 휴가가 끝날 때까지 무엇을 배우실 건가요?

By when **will** my father **have learnt** how to scuba dive?
저희 아버지께서는 언제까지 스쿠버다이빙을 배우실 건가요?

The training of new police officers **will have finished** in six months.
→ The training of new police officers **won't have finished** in six months.
신입 경찰관들을 위한 교육은 6개월 내에 끝날 것입니다. → 신입 경찰관들을 위한 교육은 6개월 내에 끝나지 않을 것입니다.

미래완료진행 Future Perfect Continuous

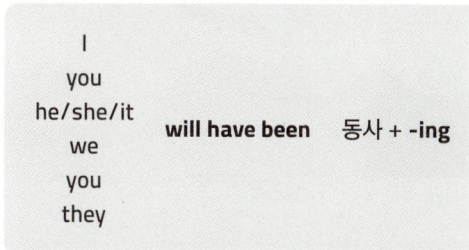

By Friday you **will have been working** with the film for a month!
금요일이 되면 당신은 한 달 동안 영화로 공부를 하고 있는 셈이 됩니다!

미래완료진행형은 미래의 종료 시점까지 행위가 지속될 때 쓰인다.

I am stranded here and I hate it. By 2 o'clock I **will have been waiting** for my plane for ten hours! 저는 이곳에 발이 묶여 있는데 정말 싫어요. 2시가 되면 10시간 동안 비행기를 기다리고 있는 셈이 되거든요!

미래완료진행: 의문문 Future Perfect Continuous: questions

Alfie **will have been driving** this car for almost ten years by the end of May.
→ Who **will have been driving** this car for almost ten years by the end of May?
Alfie는 5월 말이 되면 거의 10년째 이 차를 운전하고 있는 셈이 됩니다.
→ 5월 말이 되면 누가 거의 10년째 이 차를 운전하고 있는 셈이 되나요?

What **will** Alfie **have been driving** for almost ten years by the end of May?
5월 말이 되면 Alfie는 무엇을 10년째 운전하고 있는 셈이 되나요?

Communication situations

Read the following dialogues at the post office.

Good morning, what can I do for you?

Dialogue 1

Client: I'd like to send a letter.

Clerk: Domestic or international?

Client: International, and I'd like to send it by airmail.

Clerk: What service would you like to have it sent by?

Client: What services are available?

Clerk: We've got International Standard, International Signed, International Tracked and International Tracked and Signed.

Client: What's the difference between International Standard and International Tracked and Signed?

Clerk: With International Tracked and Signed you get priority in handling, full tracking and a signature on delivery, plus online confirmation of the delivery. These services are not available for International Standard.

Client: That's far too much. It's just a letter.

Clerk: OK. No problem.

airmail 항공 우편 I domestic 국내의 I international 국제의 I priority in handling 우선 취급

Dialogue 2

Client: I'd like to send this parcel.

Clerk: How would you like to send it? By Royal Mail or Express Service?

Client: How does Express Service work?

Clerk: Generally, the parcel is delivered next day. Depending on the chosen type of service it's on the spot at 9 a.m., 10 a.m., before noon or within 24 hours. The price depends on the weight of your parcel and the option, of course.

Client: Is the delivery guaranteed?

Clerk: Only in express48. However, in all types of Express Service your parcel is fully tracked and the signature of delivery is available online within a couple of minutes of the delivery.

Client: So what's the difference between 1st class Signed For and express48?

Clerk: The size and weight of the parcel.

Client: Thank you for the explanation. I think I'll stick to the Royal Mail after all.

Clerk: No problem.

parcel 소포 I guaranteed 보장된 I size 크기

Dialogue 3

Client: I'd like to send a letter.

Clerk: Domestic or international?

Client: It goes to Scotland.

Clerk: Well, Scotland is within the UK, so yes, domestic.

Client: OK. How much is it?

Clerk: 1st or 2nd class?

Client: What's the difference between 1st and 2nd class?

Clerk: 1st class delivery is the next working day, including Saturdays, and 2nd class within 2-3 working days. And the price is different, of course.

Client: OK. Make it 2nd class, please.

working day 근무일

Dialogue 4

Client: I'd like to send this parcel.
Clerk: How would you like to send it? By Royal Mail or Express Service?
Client: By Express Service, please.
Clerk: All right. Which option would you like?
Client: Express9, please.
Clerk: OK. Your parcel will be delivered by 9 a.m.

Dialogue 5

Client: I'd like to send this parcel.
Clerk: How would you like to send it? By Royal Mail or Express Service?
Client: Royal Mail, please.
Clerk: 1st or 2nd class?
Client: 1st class.
Clerk: Up to 1 kg it's £3.20.
Client: OK. Make it 2nd class, please.

Vocabulary plus

bubble envelope 재질이 약한 봉투

certificate of posting 우송증명서

delivery confirmation 배송 확인

jiffy bag 소포용 쿠션 봉투

stamp 우표

Cultural tips

Did you know that ...?

The **age of majority** both in the UK and U.S. is 18, except Alabama (19), Nebraska (19), Puerto Rico (21) and Mississippi (21).

The **age of consent** (the age at which a person is considered to be legally competent to consent to sexual acts) in the UK is 16. Each U.S. state has its own general age of consent. Currently state laws set the age of consent at 16, 17, or 18.

Scene 4 (40) — Film dialogue and vocabulary

Read the dialogue between Martin (M) and his uncle (U). Check the list of words and phrases below.

What's wrong?

M: … are pleased to announce that on December 7th Beatrice Campbell, daughter of Stephen and Sophie Campbell, is to marry Robert Murray, age 26, junior partner at MacKenzie law firm … What's that rubbish? What does it mean? But we'd been talking about it for days before she left. She said: "This crappy trip will not change a thing! It's just a crappy scheme my parents came up with! Please wait for me!" And now she's getting married? To a lawyer? Who the hell is this guy?

U: Martin, I never wanted to bring this up when you two were dating, but, realistically speaking …

M: What? Realistically speaking, she shouldn't get involved with a guy like me? No money, no education, child of worthless working class parents? She was above that kind of bullshit!

U: She was above this kind of bullshit when you were around! With some time on her hands, maybe she thought this through …

M: And fell for a hotshot lawyer! I can't bloody believe it!

U: Don't go, Martin! Don't! … It's pointless!

level B2

Vocabulary			
announce	발표하다, 알리다	lawyer	변호사
marry	결혼하다	realistically speaking	현실적으로 말하자면
junior partner	신입 사원, 하급 사원	worthless	쓸모없는
law firm	로펌, 법률사무소	working class	노동자 계급
rubbish	헛소리	be above	~ 이상이다
crappy	형편없는 것	bullshit	헛소리
trip	여행	think through	충분히 생각하다
scheme	계략	fall for	~에 홀딱 반하다
come up with	생각해 내다	hotshot	잘 나가는, 능력 있는
get married	결혼하다	pointless	무의미한

What should Martin's uncle do?

let Martin go
U: Please! Don't make it worse than it is!

stop Martin
U: Let her be! It won't change a thing!

Grammar explanations

과거완료진행 Past Perfect Continuous

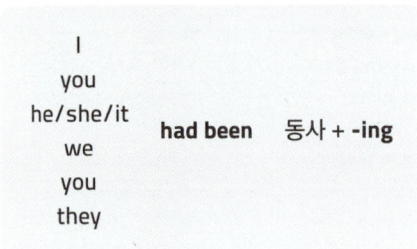

Martin **had been going** out with Beatrice before she went on the trip with her parents.
Beatrice가 부모님들과 여행을 떠나기 전에 Martin은 그녀와 함께 외출을 하고 있었습니다.

Gennady **had been working** in many countries by the time he settled down in Britain.
Gennady가 영국에 정착하기 전까지 그는 여러 나라에서 일을 했습니다.

과거완료형은 과거에 발생한 사건에 앞서 발생한 사건을 나타낸다. 반면 과거완료진행형은 과거에 발생한 사건에 앞서 계속 진행되고 있던 행위를 나타낸다.

She **had been living** in New York. 그녀는 뉴욕에 살고 있었습니다.

Before / By the time David met Olive, he **had been dating** some local girls.
David가 Olive를 만나기 전에/만나기 전까지, 그는 현지 여성들과 데이트를 하고 있었습니다.

과거완료진행: 의문문과 부정문 Past Perfect Continuous: questions and negatives

Vlad **had been doing** other jobs for Gennady before he came to London.
→ **Had** Vlad **been doing** other jobs for Gennady before he came to London?
Vlad는 영국에 오기 전에 Gennady를 위한 다른 일을 하고 있었습니다.
→ Vlad가 영국에 오기 전에 Gennady를 위한 다른 일을 하고 있었나요?

What **had** Vlad **been doing** for Gennady before he came to London?
영국에 오기 전에 Vlad는 Gennady를 위해 어떤 일을 하고 있었나요?

Who **had** Vlad **been doing** jobs for before he came to London?
영국에 오기 전에 Vlad는 누구를 위한 일을 하고 있었나요?

David **had been leading** a dramatic life before he met Olive.
→ David **hadn't been leading** a dramatic life before he met Olive.
David는 Olive를 만나기 전에 극적인 삶을 살고 있었습니다.
→ David는 Olive를 만나기 전에는 극적인 삶을 살고 있지 않았습니다.

Communication situations

Read the following dialogues from an interview with a paranormal expert.

Now, Mr Puzzle, you deal professionally with paranormal phenomena. You make documentaries and write books on the subject.

Dialogue 1

Mr Puzzle: Generally speaking, yes.

Interviewer: You must admit it's not a typical nine to five job. Could you give us the general idea about the things you deal with?

Mr Puzzle: I try to achieve the impossible: to explain things beyond human understanding.

Interviewer: So, you basically tell people what they want to hear?

Mr Puzzle: Of course not. I help people accept the unknowable and live with it.

Interviewer: And they really buy all this mumbo-jumbo?
Give me a break.

Mr Puzzle: What are you afraid of? Have you experienced something unusual?

Interviewer: Strictly off the record, you're right, I am afraid. That you might be clinically insane. Still, let's give this interview another try.

beyond human understanding 인간이 이해할 수 있는 범위를 넘어선 | **accept** 받아들이다 | **unknowable** 알 수 없는 | **mumbo-jumbo** 허튼소리 | **experience** 경험하다 | **strictly** 엄밀히 | **off the record** 비공식적으로 | **clinically insane** 의학적으로 제정신이 아닌

Dialogue 2

Interviewer: So, to put it bluntly – who the heck are you?

Mr Puzzle: I'm the one who listens and believes when everybody else closes their ears.

Interviewer: So, you basically tell people what they want to hear?

Mr Puzzle: No, I use scientific methods and tools in my work.

Interviewer: You mean a pendulum?

Mr Puzzle: Why the sarcasm? There is no need to disrespect either me or my clients.

Interviewer: All right. I apologize. It's just that your profession is quite unique.

---

to put it bluntly 솔직히 말해서 | **the heck** 도대체 | **pendulum** 추 | **disrespect** 무시하다

Dialogue 3

Mr Puzzle: I investigate all kinds of supernatural events that science cannot explain.

Interviewer: Speaking of which, in your latest book titled Around the Supernatural Globe you describe some really terrifying incidents. Let's talk about some of those now.

Mr Puzzle: What exactly would you like to talk about? UFOs? Myths and legends? Cryptozoology?

Interviewer: Could you tell us a little bit about all of them?

Mr Puzzle: Impossible! It's a very wide field, encompassing a number of complex problems.

Interviewer: I see what you mean. We could be here all day and barely scratch the surface. What a fascinating life you must lead!

---

investigate 조사하다 | **latest** 최근의 | **myths and legends** 신화와 전설 | **wide** 넓은 | **encompass** 포함하다, 아우르다 | **barely scratch the surface** 극히 일부만 다루다

Vocabulary plus

assumption 추정

Blimey! 맙소사!

common 흔한

communicate 소통하다

conventional 진부한

cover the subject 주제를 다루다

dearly departed 고인이 된

dedicated to ~에 전념하는, 헌신하는

density 밀도

documentary 다큐멘터리, 기록물

elaborate 자세히 설명하다

for instance 예를 들어

ghost 유령

give the once-over 대충 훑어보다

go in circles 헛수고하다

haunting 괴담

have a tantrum 짜증을 부리다

humidity 습도

I beg to differ. 제 생각은 조금 다릅니다.

lesser-known 별로 유명하지 않은

living fossil 살아 있는 화석

measuring air parameters 대기 변수 측정

meter 계량기

minion 부하

misconception 오해

name 이름을 대다

paranormal phenomena 초자연적인 현상들

performing monkey 공연하는 원숭이; 광대, 꼭두각시

prior permission 사전 허가

professionally 전문적으로

range 범위

relative 친척

repeatable 반복할 수 있는

space 공간

specialized 전문적인

spirit 영혼

That's no way to talk to a lady. 숙녀에게 그렇게 말하면 못 써.

thermal imaging equipment 열로 이미지를 처리하는 장비

trope 상투적인 장치

turn-up for the books 뜻밖의 상황

werewolf 늑대인간

wrongly 부당하게

Cultural tips

Did you know that …?

UFO, short for "unidentified flying object", refers to any phenomenon in the sky that cannot be identified. The term was officially created in 1953 by the United States Air Force.

Scene 5 (41) — Film dialogue and vocabulary

Read the dialogue between Murray (R), Beatrice (B) and Martin (M). Check the list of words and phrases below.

R: There, there boy! You're upsetting her! (…) You shouldn't have tried to hit me! Do you like it down there in the mud? I guess it's the position you're well accustomed to, huh? In fact, that's the root of the problem, isn't it? Your desire to climb up … But Beatrice will not help you cut corners!

B: Stop it! Leave him alone!

M: What did they do to you? They must've done something while you were gone? Tell me!

B: I'm pregnant.

R: Yes, Martin. We're expecting a baby! I do understand that there was some infatuation between the two of you, but please understand: it is over! Beatrice and I are getting married soon and I'll provide the baby with the best possible conditions. It's a lot more than you could offer, isn't it?

level B2

Vocabulary

presume	추정하다	desire	욕망
upset	당황하게 하다	cut corners	(일을 쉽게 하려고) 절차를 무시[생략]하다
hit	치다	while	~ 동안
mud	진흙	expect a baby	임신 중이다
position	자세	infatuation	(사랑의) 열병
be accustomed to	~에 익숙하다	provide	주다, 제공하다
root of the problem / root of one's problem	문제의 근원	the best possible	가능한 가장 ~ 한

Beatrice, please. This can't be true!

Grammar explanations

과거 조동사 Past modal verbs

> 추측

→ 과거에 발생한 사건에 대해 확신할 때, *must + have + 과거분사*를 사용한다.

Martin looks horrible. He **must have had** a terrible night.
(= I am sure he had a terrible night.)
Martin은 겁에 질려 보여요. 틀림없이 끔찍한 밤을 보냈을 거예요. (= 저는 그가 끔찍한 밤을 보냈다고 확신해요.)

Curtis is unconscious. Olive **must have drugged** him.
(= I believe / I'm certain that Olive drugged him.)
Curtis는 의식이 없어요. 틀림없이 Olive가 그에게 약을 먹였을 거예요. (= 저는 Olive가 그에게 약을 먹였을 것이라고 믿어요.)

→ 과거에 발생한 사건에 대한 개연성이나 가능성을 나타낼 때, *may / might / could + have + 과거분사*를 사용한다.

Robert seems very confident. He **may / might / could have drunk** some alcohol.
(= It is possible. You never know with Robert.)
Robert는 매우 자신있어 보여요. 그는 아마 술을 약간 마셨을 거예요. (= 가능한 일이에요. Robert에 대해서는 알 수 없어요.)

Curtis is unconscious. Olive **might have drugged** him.
(= Maybe she drugged him, maybe she didn't. Maybe he is just drunk – you never know with Curtis.)
Curtis는 의식이 없어요. 아마 Olive가 그에게 약을 먹였을 거예요. (= 아마 그녀가 그에게 약을 먹였을 수도 있고 먹이지 않았을 수도 있어요. 아마 취했을 수도 있어요 – Curtis에 대해서는 알 수 없어요.)

→ 과거 사건에 대한 불가능성을 나타낼 때, *can't / couldn't + have + 과거분사*를 사용한다.

Martin **can't / couldn't have planned** the encounter with Robert and Beatrice.
(= It was obviously spontaneous.)
Martin이 Robert와 Beatrice와의 만남을 계획했을 리가 없어요. (= 그것은 분명 자발적이었어요.)

Curtis is unconscious. But Olive **can't have drugged** him this time – she wasn't even at the party. Curtis는 의식이 없어요. 하지만 이번에는 Olive가 그에게 약을 먹였을 리가 없어요 – 그녀는 파티에 오지도 않았는걸요.

> 의무

➔ 과거에 해야 했던 일에 대해 말할 때, *should + have* + 과거분사를 사용한다. 과거에 이행했던 일에 대한 후회를 나타낼 때, *shouldn't + have* + 과거분사를 사용한다.

Martin **should have taken** a gun to stop Robert from humiliating him (but he didn't and it was a mistake). Martin은 자신에 대한 Robert의 모욕을 중단시키기 위해 총을 집었어야 했어요. (하지만 그러지 않았는데 그건 실수였어요.)

Curtis is unconscious. He **should have been** more careful when dealing with Olive. On the other hand, Olive **shouldn't have drugged** him – his father is a dangerous man. Curtis는 의식이 없어요. 그는 Olive를 상대할 때 보다 조심했어야 했어요. 반면, Olive는 그에게 약을 주지 말았어야 했어요 – 그의 아버지는 무서운 분이거든요.

➔ 과거에 불필요하게 이행된 일에 대해 말할 때, *needn't + have* + 과거분사를 사용한다.

Martin **needn't have tried** to hit Robert; Murray and Beatrice had already made their plans. Martin은 Robert를 때리려고 할 필요가 없었어요; Murray와 Beatrice가 이미 계획을 세워두었죠.

Curtis is unconscious. Olive **needn't have drugged** him – he took care of it himself and drank enough to sink a ship. It was a waste of a good drug. Curtis는 의식이 없어요. Olive가 그에게 약을 먹일 필요는 없었어요 – 그가 직접 나서서 배를 가라앉힐 만큼 마셨죠. 좋은 약을 허비했어요.

Communication situations

Read the following dialogues. A couple of friends are meeting without their families for a bit of gossip.

Hello love, sorry I'm late. You know, kids, kids, kids everywhere. Oh, I can see you have already ordered the apple pie. That's very wise; they've got the best apple pie in town. Anyway, where are Suzie, Clara and Jessie?

Dialogue 1

B: Hello dear. Haven't you heard?

A: Heard about what?

B: Suzie and John have broken up.

A: Oh, that's terrible news.

B: And it's my fault.

A: Come on, don't say that. I'm sure it's not your fault.

B: But it's true. I shouldn't have been so nosy.

A: Meaning?

B: I caught them both red-handed.

A: What?

B: I saw both of them kissing strangers.

A: Oh, what a mess! And what now?

B: Their divorce case is in progress.

A: Already? They should have tried marriage counselling or something. What a pity.

nosy 참견하기 좋아하는 | **catch somebody red-handed** ~을 현행범으로 붙잡다 | **divorce case** 이혼 소송 | **marriage counselling** 결혼 상담

Dialogue 2

B: Clara had to stay with the kids.

A: Well, I've got kids too and I still came.

B: Well, she feels guilty after the accident and wants to spend more time with them.

A: Accident? I haven't heard about "the accident". What happened?

B: She had a car collision when she was taking the children to school.

A: Oh no! Are they OK?

B: Physically yes, but the children still get anxious when someone mentions a car.

A: They are still traumatized. Sad to say, but it may last a bit until they get better.

collision 충돌 | **physically** 신체적으로 | **be traumatized** 정신적인 충격을 받다 | **sad to say, but ...** 유감스럽게도 ...

Dialogue 3

B: Clara has gone to India.

A: To India? What for?

B: To become a Buddhist.

A: What do you mean?

B: Well, she met this guy 3 months ago.

A: And who is the lucky guy?

B: Her yoga teacher.

A: Oh yes, I should have guessed that.

Vocabulary plus

assistance 도움

at the end of the day 결국

babysit 아이를 봐 주다

bark up the wrong tree
잘못 짚다, 엉뚱한 사람을 비난하다

be a perfect match 잘 어울리는 커플이다

call names 욕을 하다

cheer up 격려하다

cliché 진부한 표현

eager 열렬한

early bird 일찍 일어나는 사람

enter into wedlock 결혼하다

feel sorry for 가엾게 여기다

flat (타이어에) 바람이 빠진, 펑크가 난

foresee 예견하다

get on well (남들과) 잘 지내다

go wrong 잘못되다

grounded 외출 금지된

have a crush on ~에게 홀딱 반하다

leg 다리

man eater 남성 편력이 심한 여자

mother-in-law 시어머니, 장모

mummy 엄마 (아이들이 쓰는 말)

nanny 유모

night owl 올빼미 같은 사람

pneumonia 폐렴

put it this way 이렇게 설명하다

sensitive 민감한

Shit happens. 불운한 상황이 일어나기 마련이다.

sister-in-law 형수, 제수, 시누이, 올케

start a rumour 소문을 내기 시작하다

stubborn 고집스러운

surely 확실히

twist one's ankle 발목을 삐다

tyre 타이어

weather conditions 기상 조건

Cultural tips

Did you know that ...?

An apple pie is a fruit pie, in which the main ingredient is apple. It can be served with whipped cream or ice cream on top, or together with cheddar cheese.

Scene 6 (42) Film dialogue and vocabulary

Read the dialogue between Martin (M) and his uncle (U). Check the list of words and phrases below.

M: I have. Murray's done it! Accomplished what he's been planning all along! I just wish I'd recognized sooner how vile he is. I could have tried harder to save her!

U: I don't understand? What … What are you suggesting?

M: Suggesting? I know. Robert Murray has murdered Beatrice's parents. Now there is no-one to stop him from stealing her money. Bit by bit, one legal trick after another …

U: You've got no proof! And forgive me for saying this, but you went bonkers when you lost her to him. I'd rather you came back here so I can help you stand on your own two feet.

M: Thank you, but I'm alright. I've been taking night shifts and studying during the day, you know, keeping myself busy.

U: I'm glad you're picking up the pieces. But if you need money, just ask me.

M: I do, but not the sort of money you can offer me. To take on a man like Murray, one needs enormous funds and some leverage. And I'll get all that, but it'll take some time.

U: Martin, this doesn't sound sane. I think it'd be a good idea for me to come to London, talk to you.

M: There is no need for that!

level B2

Vocabulary

accomplish	성취하다, 이루다	would rather	~하면 좋겠다
plan	계획하다	stand on one's own two feet	자립하다
recognise	알다	night shift	야간근무
vile	비열한, 야비한	pick up the pieces	(안 좋은 일을 겪은 후) 정상으로 돌아가다
suggest	제안하다	take on	~를 상대하다
bit	조금, 약간	funds	자금
trick	속임수	leverage	영향력, 수단
proof	증거	sane	제정신인
forgive	용서하다		
go bonkers	미치다		

What should Martin's uncle do?

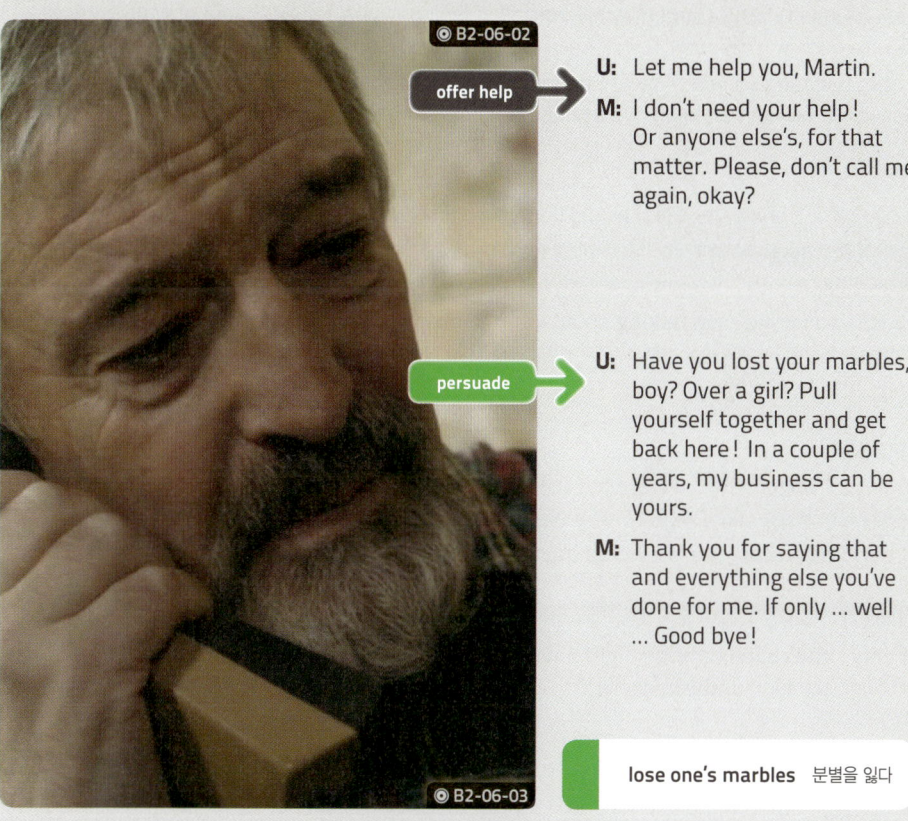

B2-06-02

offer help
U: Let me help you, Martin.
M: I don't need your help! Or anyone else's, for that matter. Please, don't call me again, okay?

persuade
U: Have you lost your marbles, boy? Over a girl? Pull yourself together and get back here! In a couple of years, my business can be yours.
M: Thank you for saying that and everything else you've done for me. If only … well … Good bye!

B2-06-03

lose one's marbles	분별을 잃다

level B2 Scene 6 (42)

Grammar explanations

Wish

wish는 현재 혹은 과거에 대한 후회를 나타낸다.
현재에 대한 후회를 나타낼 때 단순과거시제를 함께 쓴다.

I **wish** I **was** a brave man! (but I am not and I am sorry about it)
제가 용감한 사람이면 좋겠어요! (하지만 저는 용감하지 않고 그래서 유감이에요.)

I **wish** I **had** more money with me now. (but I don't and I am not happy with it)
지금 제게 돈이 더 많이 있으면 좋겠어요. (하지만 제게 돈이 많지가 않아서 행복하지 않아요.)

과거에 대한 후회를 나타낼 때 과거완료시제를 함께 쓴다.

I **wish** I **hadn't argued** with my parents yesterday. (but I did and I regret it)
어제 부모님과 싸우지 않았더라면 좋았을 거예요. (하지만 싸웠고 후회하고 있어요.)

I **wish** I **had studied** harder when I was at school. (but I didn't and school is over)
학교 다닐 때 공부를 더 열심히 했더라면 좋았을 거예요. (하지만 하지 않았고 학교 생활은 끝났어요.)

wish가 들어간 문장에서는 I/he/she/it이 주어 자리에 오더라도 was/wasn't 대신에 were/weren't를 쓸 수 있다. 그러나 후자의 경우, 보다 격식을 차린 표현이어서 상대적으로 덜 사용된다.

I **wish** I **was** taller. I could play basketball. = I **wish** I **were** taller. I could play basketball.
키가 더 크면 좋았을 거예요. 농구를 할 수 있을 거예요.

I **wish** it **wasn't** so late! We are never going to make it now!
= I **wish** it **weren't** so late! We are never going to make it now!
너무 늦지 않았다면 좋았을 거예요! 이제는 시간에 맞춰 갈 수가 없어요!

wish가 들어간 문장에서는 조동사 would가 미래를 나타내지 않고, 타인의 행동에 대한 비판을 나타낸다.

I **wish** my **neighbours wouldn't play** loud music in the middle of the night. It is very annoying! 이웃들이 한밤 중에 시끄러운 음악을 틀지 않으면 좋겠어요. 너무 짜증이 나요!

I **wish** **you would stop** talking about your last trip to Sicily. We have heard it hundreds of times. 지난번 시실리 여행에 대한 이야기는 그만하면 좋겠어요. 수백 번 들었으니까요.

If only

if only는 I wish와 비슷한 의미를 지녔지만, 더 강하고 극단적이다.

현재에 대한 후회를 나타낼 때는 if only + 단순과거

If only I **had** a car! My life would be much easier! (but I don't have a car)
제게 차가 한 대 있다면! 아내가 훨씬 편하겠죠! (하지만 차가 없어요.)

과거에 대한 후회를 나타낼 때는 if only + 과거완료

If only I **had called** him the night before! I would have spared him a lot of problems!
(I didn't call him, unfortunately) 제가 그 전날 밤에 그에게 전화를 했더라면! 그가 많은 문제를 겪지 않았을 거예요!
(안타깝게도 저는 그에게 전화를 하지 않았어요.)

It's (high/about) time

it's (high/about) time은 긴박한 상황이나 시간의 부족을 강조하며, 두 가지 구조로 사용될 수 있다.

It's (high/about) time + 사람 + 단순과거

It's time we **talked** about it.
지금이 바로 우리가 그것에 대해 이야기해야 할 때예요.

It's high time you **started** learning!
지금이 바로 당신이 공부를 시작할 때예요!

It's about time Jack **moved** on with the project.
지금이 바로 Jack이 프로젝트를 수행해야 할 때예요.

It's (high/about) time + *for* + 사람 + to부정사

It's time for us **to talk** about it.
지금이 바로 우리가 그것에 대해 이야기해야 할 때예요.

It's high time for you **to start** learning!
지금이 바로 당신이 공부를 시작할 때예요!

It's about time for Jack **to move** on with the project.
지금이 바로 Jack이 프로젝트를 수행해야 할 때예요.

I'd rather

I'd rather은 본인의 선호를 나타내며, 이 경우 동사의 원형이 뒤따른다.

I'd rather take the dog for a walk.
개를 데리고 산책을 하고 싶군요.

I'd rather think about holidays.
휴가에 대해 생각해 보고 싶군요.

I'd rather repeat what they have to do.
그들이 해야 하는 일을 다시 한 번 말하고 싶군요.

I'd rather은 타인에 대한 선호를 나타낼 수도 있는데, 이 경우 단순과거시제가 뒤따른다.

I'd rather you took the dog for a walk.
당신이 개를 데리고 산책을 하는 것이 좋겠어요.

I'd rather we thought about holidays.
우리가 휴가에 대해 생각해 보는 것이 좋겠어요.

I'd rather you repeated what they have to do.
그들이 해야 하는 일을 당신이 다시 한 번 말하는 것이 좋겠어요.

Communication situations

Read the following dialogues between friends. One of them has been through a lot recently.

That's just not fair. All those years! I sacrificed my hobbies, my career, well - myself, and for what?

Dialogue 1

Friend: I know, but calm down, dear, you'll hurt yourself.

Ex-wife: I can't, it really shook me up! We have been … Sorry - we were – together for 25 years and then my marriage was terminated after a 10-minute divorce trial.

Friend: Take it as a chance for a new life.

Ex-wife: But I liked the old one. Even loved it. I was happy.

Friend: But he obviously wasn't. Still, there's no point in looking backwards.

Ex-wife: How can you be so cruel when I can neither face the past nor look to the future?

Friend: My dear, your marriage simply ran its course. It's time to move on.

Ex-wife: Perhaps … But what's next? What do I do now? I'm in pieces.

divorce trial 이혼 재판 | **look backwards** 되돌아보다 | **look to the future** 장래를 바라보다 | **run its course** 자연스럽게 끝이 나다 | **be in pieces** 산산조각 나다

Dialogue 2

Friend: Life can be really unfair sometimes.

Widow: Sometimes, you say? Life is always unfair!

Friend: I know. It must be very hard for you now.

Widow: Yes, it is.

Friend: Excuse my asking, but is it because of the loss or because of the publication of his will?

Widow: He had been sick for months. It's the will that made me furious. He wrote it over 15 years ago.

Friend: Now I'm beginning to understand …

Widow: Yes. That woman is one of the beneficiaries even though they hadn't been married for years.

Friend: But as far as I know, you can't disinherit your current spouse.

Widow: I know, but still! That's just ridiculous! He should have done something about it, not leave me to deal with his decade-old liabilities.

---

unfair 불공평한 | **will** 유언(장) | **disinherit** 상속권을 박탈하다 | **spouse** 배우자 | **liability** 골칫거리

Dialogue 3

Friend: I know. It must be very hard for you now.

Widow: Yes, it is.

Friend: He was a wonderful person. And you took care of him with such love!

Widow: Yet after all those years together he left me with nothing.

Friend: I'm not sure if it's the right time to talk about his will.

Widow: When will the time be right then? After all those distant relatives have made away with his fortune?

Friend: Come on, he had the right to appoint the beneficiaries.

Widow: But where the hell were they all those years when his health was failing? Bloodsuckers, the lot of them.

---

wonderful 멋진 | **make away with** ~를 가지고 떠나다 | **appoint the beneficiaries** 상속인을 지명하다 | **bloodsucker** 남의 고혈을 빼먹는 사람

Vocabulary plus

at-fault divorce 당사자 쌍방의 책임을 묻는 이혼
attempts 시도
be on speaking terms
(특히 언쟁을 벌인 후) ~와 사이 좋게 말을 하다
behavior 행동
bequeath (유언으로) 양도하다
bimbo 백치 미인
celebrate 기념하다
child custody 자녀 양육권
commodity 상품
cut all ties with ~와 인연을 끊다
deal a heavy blow 큰 타격을 주다
deliberate 숙고하다
devise to (유언으로) 양도하다
dispose of ~을 처리하다
divide 나누다
exclude 제외하다
executor 유언 집행자
forgery 위조품
give somebody a run for their money
~와 대적하다
greedy 탐욕스러운
grieve 비통해 하다
have to spare 여분이 있다
heiress 상속녀
honest 정직한
in black and white 글로
in the first place 우선
inheritance law 상속법
initiate 시작하다
It takes two. 손뼉도 마주쳐야 소리가 난다.
lamentable 한탄스러운

leave penniless 무일푼으로 남겨두다
lion's share 가장 큰 몫
malicious 악의적인
marital property 부부 재산
mediated 중재된, 조정된
no-fault divorce 당사자 쌍방의 책임을 묻지 않는 이혼
on top of everything else 설상가상으로
owner 주인
possession 소유(물)
practical 현실적인
prenuptial agreement 혼전 합의서
probate proceeding 공증 절차
rage 격노
rub salt into the wound 사태를 더 악화시키다
rule 판결을 내리다
sacrifice 희생하다
serve one right 당연하다, 꼴좋다
shake up (마음을) 뒤흔들다
significant 상당한
sole heir 유일한 상속인
solicitor 사무 변호사
spare (불쾌한 일을) 모면하게 하다
spy on ~를 염탐하다
sue for ~를 청구하다, ~에 대한 소송을 걸다
tend to ~하는 경향이 있다
ugly 못생긴
uncontested divorce 소송의 여지가 없는 이혼
vulture 독수리; (약한 자를 희생시키는) 무자비하고 욕심 많은 사람; 사기꾼
wash one's dirty linen 내부[집안]의 수치를 밖으로 드러내다

Cultural tips

Did you know that ...?

A person's "marital status" is the answer to the question about whether he or she is married. This question is usually seen on the forms that require you to give basic personal data. The application forms may ask you to select either the word "single" or "married".

Scene 7 (43) — Film dialogue and vocabulary

Read the dialogue between a man (M) and Olive (O). Check the list of words and phrases below.

Miss, are you all right?

M: Do you need help? Do you have a medical condition? Shall I call an ambulance?
O: I'm okay.
M: Are you … Are you on medication? It looks as if you've been drugged by someone!
O: Can't deny that!
M: Have you been robbed or abused in any way? If so, I strongly suggest calling the police!
O: I probably deserved to have been treated like that!
M: How can you say that? You're not to be blamed for what … they did to you!
O: What? No! I haven't been abused. Look, I appreciate your trying to help me, but I'm all right! I just need a moment alone to figure out what to do, okay? (…) Wait! I do feel a bit dizzy. Do you have a car somewhere nearby? I might need to be taken to hospital. Oh no! My wallet! I dropped it under the bench! I need to go back and …

level B2

Vocabulary				
	medical condition	질병, 질환	treat	대하다
	ambulance	구급차	blame (for)	~에 대해 비난하다
	medication	약	appreciate	감사히 여기다
	deny	부정하다	figure out	생각해 내다
	rob	털다, 도둑질하다	feel dizzy	현기증을 느끼다
	abuse	추행하다	nearby	인근에
	strongly	강하게	bench	벤치

Look, look, look. You stay here! I'll go and fetch it, okay? Don't worry! It won't take a minute!

Grammar explanations

부정사/동명사를 취하는 동사 Verbs with infinitive and gerund

→ 대부분의 동사는 to부정사를 취한다.

David **would like to come** back to normal life in Old Berry, but such wishes don't come true easily. David는 Old Berry에서 다시 정상적인 생활을 하고 싶어 했지만, 그런 바람은 쉽게 실현되지 않아요.

Sergey **promised to help** Vlad if it involved nothing brutal.
Sergey는 잔인한 것과 관련이 없는 일이라면 Vlad를 돕겠다고 약속했어요.

This **seems to be** a misunderstanding. How can you not like Olive Green?
이것은 오해처럼 보여요. 어떻게 Olive Green을 좋아하지 않을 수 있죠?

Olive **managed to survive** the fight in the dungeon, although it was a narrow escape.
비록 간신히 빠져 나오기는 했지만 Olive는 지하 감옥에서의 싸움에서 살아남을 수 있었어요.

Jessica **hopes to find** the right woman for her son. Jessica는 아들에게 꼭 맞는 여성을 찾고 싶어해요.

David secretly **agreed to work** for Robert Murray. David는 비밀에 Robert Murray를 위해 일하겠다고 동의했어요.

to부정사를 취하는 그밖의 동사: expect, happen, learn, offer, plan, pretend, refuse, tend, threaten, want

→ 동명사(동사 + -ing)를 취하는 동사

In the middle of the whole confusion with Olive and the Russian gangsters David suddenly began to **miss doing** his boring job.
Olive와 러시아 갱들에 대해 혼란스러워 하던 도중에 David는 갑자기 자신의 지루한 일이 그리워지기 시작했어요.

As Murray **kept talking**, David understood he had no choice but to work for him.
Murray가 계속 이야기를 했기 때문에 David는 그를 위해 일하는 것 이외에는 다른 선택권이 없다는 점을 알고 있었어요.

Olive just can't **avoid running** into trouble on a regular basis.
Olive는 규칙적으로 발생하는 문제와 대면하는 일을 피할 수 없어요.

Vlad **didn't mind doing** some dirty work for Gennady.
Vlad는 Gennady를 위한 것이라면 더러운 일도 마다하지 않았어요.

He was a ruthless man and **enjoyed roughing** people up.
그는 무자비한 사람이었고 사람들을 폭행하는 것을 즐겼어요.

He **couldn't help starting** a fight every now and then. 그는 때때로 싸움을 시작하지 않을 수 없었어요.

동명사를 취하는 그밖의 동사: deny, fancy, finish, imagine, risk, suggest

→ 원형부정사를 취하는 조동사

At first David's mother **didn't let** him **study** at the police academy.
처음에 David의 어머니는 그가 경찰 학교에서 공부하는 것을 허락하지 않았어요.

She wanted him to **help** her **run** the B&B. 그녀는 그가 자신을 도와 B&B를 운영하기를 원했어요.

She even tried to **make** him **study** tourism! 그녀는 심지어 그에게 관광학을 공부시키려고 했어요!

David, however, **would rather do** something that made more sense to him.
하지만 David는 자신에게 보다 적합한 무언가를 하고 싶어 했어요.

He **had better help** the community and **bring** order everywhere if he could!
그는 지역 사회를 돕고 가능한 모든 곳에 질서를 가져다 주어야 해요!

He felt he **should help** people and that he **could do** it.
그는 자신이 사람들을 도와야 하고 또 그렇게 할 수 있다고 생각했어요.

→ 동명사는 절을 축약시킬 수 있다.

Do you **mind if I open** the window? → Do you **mind me/my* opening** the window?
제가 창문을 열어도 될까요?

I **appreciate it that you came** to the meeting. → I **appreciate you/your* coming** to the meeting.   모임에 와 주신다면 고맙겠습니다.

*동명사로 축약이 이루어진 절에서는 목적격대명사(*me, him, us* etc.) 혹은 소유격대명사(*my, your, his* etc.)를 사용한다.

As if / As though

말하는 내용을 사실이라고 믿는 경우, **as if / as though**절 안에 단순현재, 현재완료와 같은 현재시제를 쓴다.
He looks **as if / as though** he **is** an MI-5 agent. (he has got sunglasses, a suit and a toy gun)   그는 마치 MI-5 요원처럼 보여요. (그는 선글라스, 정장, 그리고 장난감 총을 가지고 있어요.)

She speaks **as if / as though** she **has been** there before. (she shows genuine knowledge)
그녀는 마치 그곳에 있었던 것처럼 말을 해요. (그녀는 제대로 알고 있어요.)

말하는 내용에 대한 사실 여부가 불명확할 경우, **as if / as though**절 안에 단순과거, 과거완료와 같은 과거시제를 쓴다.
He looks **as if / as though** he **was** an MI-5 agent. (but the guy is probably not an agent)
그는 마치 MI-5 요원처럼 보여요. (하지만 그 남자는 아마도 요원이 아닐 거예요.)

She speaks **as if / as though** she **had been** there before. (she probably hasn't visited the place)   그녀는 마치 그곳에 있었던 것처럼 말을 해요. (그녀는 아마 그곳에 가 보지 못했을 거예요.)

Communication situations

Read the following dialogues between one of the tenants and an employee of the administration.

Hello, good morning. Please, have a seat. How can I help you?

Dialogue 1

Tenant: Hello, there is a problem with my bathroom.
Employee: All right. Is it about the shower, the bath or the toilet?
Tenant: It's the frigging bath.
Employee: I see. Could you describe the problem?
Tenant: I think there is a blockage in my trap.
Employee: Oh, in that case your trap will have to be dismantled.
Tenant: When can a plumber visit me?
Employee: Tomorrow is possible if that's fine with you.

bathroom 욕실 ǀ shower 샤워기; 샤워 ǀ bath 욕조 ǀ toilet 변기 ǀ frigging 빌어먹을 ǀ blockage (흐름을) 막는 것 ǀ trap 배수관 ǀ dismantle 분해하다 ǀ plumber 배관공

Olive Green

Dialogue 2

Tenant: I'd like to speak to the property manager.

Employee: You're in the office of the property manager. We are all here to help you in case of a problem. So, is there something wrong?

Tenant: I think I have flooded my downstairs neighbour.

Employee: Oh no ... Do you have insurance?

Tenant: I don't but he does.

Employee: All right. So he's the lucky guy here.

Tenant: What do you mean?

Employee: Well, in all likelihood the insurance will cover the loss but then the insurance company will make a claim to cover the cost.

Tenant: So one way or the other it's on me.

Employee: Unfortunately yes.

---

property manager 시설 관리자 | **flood** 물에 잠기게하다; 범람시키다 | **in all likelihood** 십중팔구 | **make a claim** 청구하다

Dialogue 3

Tenant: There was a power cut in the morning and since then I have been without electricity.

Employee: That's weird. We haven't been informed about any power cut. And there hasn't been a single report on that from other residents. Are you sure you've paid the bill?

Tenant: Excuse me?

Employee: Well, people sometimes forget to pay the bills, that's why I'm asking.

Tenant: Yes, of course I have.

Employee: OK. Let's try to arrange a visit from an electrician.

Tenant: But I'm about to go away for a couple of days and there will be nobody at home.

Employee: Don't worry. You can leave the keys with us and it will be fixed when you are back.

Tenant: I'd rather be at home when somebody comes.

Employee: OK, in that case please fill in this availability form and we'll make a match with a repairman.

---

electricity 전기 | **electrician** 전기 기사 | **fix** 수리하다 | **make a match** 짝을 맞추다 | **repairman** 수리공

Vocabulary plus

accidentally 우연히

be obliged 해야 한다

blocked 차단된

candle 양초

cistern 물탱크

clog 막히다

drain 배수관, 빠져나가다

flush tank 저수 탱크

get stuck 막히다, 꼼짝 못하게 되다

in darkness 어둠 속에

limescale 물때

maintenance 유지

permanent 영구적인

potential 잠재적인

prepayment 선불

pressure 압력

rim 가장자리

shower head 샤워 꼭지

snake 하수관 청소용 와이어

sponge 스펀지

suit ~에게 편리하다

swipe card 전자 카드

token 토큰

top up ~를 보충하다; 한도를 늘리다

unscrew 열다

Cultural tips

Did you know that ...?

When you call 999, an operator will ask you which emergency service you need. In a medical emergency, ask for the ambulance service and you will be put through to one of the call-takers. You will need to have the following information available when you call 999:
+ The location where you are, including the area or postcode;
+ The phone number you are calling from;
+ Exactly what has happened.

You will also be asked to give some extra information, including:
+ The patient's age, gender and medical history;
+ Whether the patient is awake/conscious, breathing and if there is any serious bleeding or chest pain;
+ Details of the injury and how it happened.

Scene 8 (44)   Film dialogue and vocabulary

Read Olive's monologue. Check the list of words and phrases below.

You're not answering my phone calls, so I don't know where you are … But somehow I feel you're not far away. Look, I need those documents badly. You must understand one thing. And maybe if I'd told you that earlier, we'd have taken a different path, but what can I say? I do have trust issues.

But I digress! The transaction that's about to happen this evening … I'm not doing it for money! I'm not, okay? The man who hired me went to great lengths to find out who I really am. He's in a position to hurt a member of my family … My mom. I do believe he'd do that. He still might.

It's a mess, I admit. I've been forced to take part in some sick game between that guy and Murray. I am really sorry I dragged you into this.

If I'd known all this a few weeks ago, I'd have chosen a different B&B in Old Berry. Though, I'm not sure there are any other to choose from.

I've managed to get in touch with the client. We're meeting in an hour. Since I don't have the documents, there's only one solution that comes to mind!

It's a very risky solution, and one that I detest. Anyway, I'll text you the address of the place. If you're there with the documents, then who knows, we might have a normal date, you and I. If you're not there, I won't hold it against you.

level B2

Vocabulary

phone call	전화	drag (into)	~을 끌어들이다
early	일찍	choose	고르다
path	길, (인생의) 행로	manage (to)	간신히 ~하다
digress	주제에서 벗어나다	since	~ 때문에
go to great lengths	많은 애를 쓰다	come to mind	생각이 떠오르다
force	억지로 ~시키다	detest	몹시 싫어하다
take part (in)	참여하다, 가담하다	text	문자를 보내다
game	계략, 수작	hold against	~를 원망하다

Goodbye, David.

Grammar explanations

가정법 과거완료 Third Conditional

if + 사람 + **had done**, 사람 + **would have done**

사람 + **would have done** **if** + 사람 + **had done**

If Olive **had been** more careful, she **wouldn't have made** a good art thief in the past.
Olive가 보다 신중했더라면 그녀는 과거에 뛰어난 미술품 도둑이 되지는 않았을 거예요.

David **wouldn't have asked** Olive out if she **hadn't acted** so mysteriously when they met in Old Berry.
Old Berry에서 만났을 때 그녀가 그처럼 의심스럽게 행동하지 않았다면 David는 Olive에게 나가라고 하지 않았을 거예요.

If David **hadn't been** so law-abiding, he **wouldn't have become** a police officer in the past.
David가 그처럼 법을 준수하는 사람이 아니었다면 그는 과거에 경찰관이 되지 않았을 거예요.

Jessica **wouldn't have kept** looking for a girl for her son if he **had had** more luck with women before he met Olive.
Olive를 만나기 전에 여성을 만날 운을 가지고 있었다면 Jessica는 아들을 위한 여성을 찾지 않았을 거예요

강조의 *do* Emphasis with *do*

조동사 do, does와 did는 문장의 의미를 강조하기 위해 사용된다.

I **do** care for you. = I **really** care for you. 저는 당신을 정말 좋아해요.

He **does** appreciate the situation. = He **really** appreciates the situation.
그는 정말로 상황을 파악했어요.

He **did** stand on his own two feet. = He **really** stood on his own two feet.
그는 정말로 자립을 했어요.

그러나 be 혹은 조동사 have가 이미 쓰인 문장에서는 조동사에 강세를 둠으로써 문장의 의미를 강조한다.

It **is** difficult for Olive to explain the situation to David.
Olive가 David에게 상황을 설명하는 것은 쉽지 않아요.

David **has** tried to understand it.
David는 그것을 이해하려고 노력했어요.

Communication situations

Read the following dialogues. Some friends are talking about their successes and failures at work.

Hi, I'm calling back. Sorry, I couldn't talk in the morning. You seemed to be very upset. What's wrong?

Dialogue 1

B: Well, I got a promotion. I've jumped onto the managerial level.
A: Congratulations! Isn't it what you have dreamt of?
B: Yes, finally. And there are going to be some changes.
A: I bet there are. Would you let me in on the secret?
B: OK. I'm going to reduce the red tape and increase the efficiency of day-to-day work.
A: You sound like a big fish already.
B: I'm going to be one so you'd better start getting used to it.
A: Please tell me that you're kidding right now …
B: Well, if I make people work better, it will bring mutual benefits.
A: … for the workers and for the company.
B: Yes, exactly!
A: Oh my God, you've been brainwashed!

promotion 승진 | **let in on the secret** 비밀을 알리다 | **reduce** 줄이다 | **increase** 증진시키다 | **day-to-day** 그날그날의 |
big fish 거물 | **get used to** ~에 익숙해지다 | **benefit** 이익; 이익이 되다 | **mutual benefits** 상호 이익

Dialogue 2

B: I'm so excited I have to talk to somebody.

A: OK. I'm listening.

B: I got an internship in Australia!

A: And you think it's good news?

B: Of course! I can already feel I've hit it big!

A: OK. Congratulations then. Why do you think they chose you?

B: Well, if I hadn't been so motivated, I wouldn't have had such positive results.

A: Oh yes, your attitude was definitely one of the reasons.

B: Are you implying something?

A: There have been some rumours about this internship and about working conditions there. I'm afraid you were the only one who was so eager to take part in it.

excited 신이 난, 흥분한 | **attitude** 태도 | **hit it big** 성공하다 | **motivated** 동기 부여된 | **positive** 긍정적인, 확신하는 | **imply** 암시하다

Dialogue 3

B: The worst scenario at work has come true.

A: Let me guess. The reorganization process is about to start.

B: Yes and I think I have to take the final decision.

A: Bravo! And what's the final decision?

B: I think it's high time I started my own business.

A: Are you sure it's the best solution?

B: If I don't try now, there might not be a second chance.

A: Surely you are right here.

B: And if it doesn't work out, I will look for another job.

A: Oh, let's be optimistic. Have you made some decisions? What market would you like to enter?

B: I want to retrain and start from scratch.

scenario 시나리오 | **be about to start** 막 시작하려는 참이다 | **work out** (일이) 잘 풀리다 | **retrain** 재교육을 받다[하다]

Vocabulary plus

advantage 유리한 점

atmosphere 공기, 분위기

be dying to know 알고 싶어 죽겠다

be fired 해고되다

beat the competition 경쟁에서 이기다

confirm suspicions 혐의를 굳히다

determination 투지, 결정

direction 방향

disappoint 실망시키다

e-commerce 전자 상거래

effectively 효과적으로

entering the market 시장 진입

For God's sake! 제발!

for one's own sake ~를 위해

frighten 겁먹게 하다

get at ~에 이르다

give up 포기하다

hesitate 망설이다

lemon 레몬

meet deadline 기한을 맞추다

niche (시장의) 틈새

one-way ticket 편도 승차권

otherwise 그렇지 않으면

owe ~ 덕분이다

persuade 설득하다

proposition (특히 사업상의) 제의

squeeze 짜내다, 압박하다

think alike 똑같이 생각하다

voluntary work 자원봉사

win (노력의 대가로서) 얻다

wisely 현명하게

Cultural tips

Did you know that ...?

Australia is an English-speaking country in the southern hemisphere between the Pacific Ocean and the Indian Ocean. Its official name is the Commonwealth of Australia. Australia is the sixth biggest country in the world by landmass. Canberra is the capital city of Australia, whereas Sydney is its biggest city. The Australian flag has a blue background, the Union Jack and six stars. The Australian coat of arms has two animals: the emu and kangaroo.

The photo shows the skyline of Sydney.

Scene 9 (45)   Film dialogue and vocabulary

Read the dialogue between Willis (W) and Olive (O). Check the list of words and phrases below.

W: Yes. Does this surprise you? Am I in danger?

O: You never know.

W: My personal safety is meaningless. What matters is an old score yet to be settled. So, I'd very much like to receive the documents you have for me!

What should Olive do?

Vocabulary		
	surprise	놀라게 하다
	be in danger	위험에 처하다
	safety	안전
	meaningless	의미 없는
	settle a score	원한을 갚다
	receive	받다

Olive Green

level **B2**

O: Look, I've run into some difficulties and I need more time to get them! A day or two …

W: That's most unfortunate, Olive! You leave me no choice but to punish you … by making the people you love suffer! Your mother for starters!

O: Please, no! I beg you!

Game over.
Try again.

Vocabulary			
run into difficulties	난관에 봉착하다	suffer	고통받다
unfortunate	불운한, 유감스러운	For starters …	우선 첫째로 …
punish	벌주다		

O: My partner will bring them … As soon as I check the money!

W: Oh yes, I did promise you that this would be profitable, didn't I? (…) You don't seem to be particularly overwhelmed! Why do I have a feeling that you're merely trying to buy some time? Does that mean you haven't got the documents?

O: I don't, but …

W: Such a disappointment! I never expected you to fail me like that!

O: Look, there's no need for you to make any rash decisions!

W: Don't worry! I'm not going to kill anyone. I'm not like Murray. I'd like to think that I'm at least morally superior to that son of a bitch!

M: Martin Willis and Miss Green – plotting together! Hardly a shocker, I'm afraid!

Vocabulary			
check	확인하다	rash decision	성급한 결정
profitable	이익이 되는, 수익성이 있는	morally	도덕적으로
particularly	특히, 유별나게	superior to	~보다 우월한
overwhelmed with	~에 압도된	son of a bitch	빌어먹을 자식
merely	단지	plot (against)	(~에 대해) 음모를 꾸미다
fail	실패하다; 실망시키다	shocker	충격을 주는 것

level B2 Scene 9 (45)

Grammar explanations

접미사 Word building - suffixes

→ 적절한 어미를 이용하여 동사를 명사로 만들 수 있다.
  - -ment 예) judge – judge**ment**
  - -ion 예) confuse – confus**ion**
  - -y 예) deliver – deliver**y**
  - -ance/-ence 예) exist – exist**ence**, resist – resist**ance**
  - -ist 예) cycle – cycl**ist**
  - -ure 예) create – creat**ure**

→ 적절한 어미를 이용하여 명사를 형용사로 만들 수 있다.
  - -al 예) magic – magic**al**
  - -ic 예) economy – econom**ic**
  - -ive 예) sense – sensit**ive**
  - -ous 예) glory – glori**ous**
  - -ate 예) accuracy – accur**ate**

→ 특징을 강조하기 위해 –**ful**을 사용한다.
  meaning**ful**, truth**ful**, care**ful**
  특징의 결핍을 나타내기 위해 –**less**를 사용한다.
  merci**less**, meaning**less**, penni**less**
  care 혹은 meaning과 같은 몇몇 명사는 위 두 종류의 어미를 모두 취할 수 있다.

→ 일반적인 명사 접미사
  - -ness 예) sad – sad**ness**
  - -ity 예) creative – creativ**ity**
  - -ance 예) important – import**ance**
  - -hood 예) child – child**hood**
  - -ship 예) dictator – dictator**ship**

→ 일반적인 동사 접미사
-en 예) short – short**en**
-ify 예) intense – intens**ify**
-ise/-ize 예) computer – computer**ise**

→ 일반적인 형용사 접미사
-ible 예) digest – digest**ible**
-ish 예) child – child**ish**
-ory 예) explain – explanat**ory**

접두사 Word building - prefixes
→ 일반적인 접두사 (대부분 부정의 의미를 나타낸다)
dis- 예) courage – **dis**courage
mis- 예) spell – **mis**spell
un- 예) believable – **un**believable
in- 예) correct – **in**correct
im- 예) possible – **im**possible
il- 예) legal – **il**legal
ir- 예) regular – **ir**regular

복합명사 Compound nouns
- 분리된 두 단어 예) **fox hunting, art collection**
- 분리되지 않은 짧은 두 단어 예) **schoolgirl, landslide, toothache**
- 매우 드물게는 하이픈과 함께 쓰이기도 한다. 예) **self-destruction**

Communication situations

Read the following dialogues between some managers at a company meeting.

Good morning everyone and thanks for coming. Today we've got a five-point agenda; however, there is an issue we have to begin with. John, the floor is yours.

Dialogue 1

John: Thank you. To put it bluntly, we have a problem with our main supplier.

Ann: Excuse me, didn't we cover this issue last month?

John: Indeed, we talked about it but we didn't reach a conclusion.

Ann: All right. Let's address the problem once more.

John: We've been badly affected by their new price list and we want to terminate our cooperation.

Ann: So why are we bringing up this issue again?

John: Because the rest of the agenda is really dull.

Ann: That's not as funny as you think it is.

John: Because they have been our business partners for years.

Ann: You might have a point there. Breaking up business relations overnight may not be beneficial for us. What do you suggest?

John: Why don't we sit down at the bargaining table again and try to get to the bottom of things.

Ann: I don't think it will help, to be honest, but if you want to try, go ahead.

---

bluntly 직설적으로 | **reach a conclusion** 결론에 도달하다 | **address the problem** 문제를 다루다 | **affected by** ~의해 영향을 받은 | **price list** 가격표, 정가표 | **bring up** (화제를) 꺼내다 | **dull** 따분한 | **relations** 관계 | **overnight** 하룻밤 사이에 | **bargaining** 협상 | **get to the bottom** 진상을 파악하다

Dialogue 2

John: Thank you. As you may all well know, there have been clashes between trade unions and the board.

Ann: Yes, indeed. We are in a dilemma over firing people or lowering their remuneration.

John: Why don't we tackle the problem differently.

Ann: That's interesting. Go on.

John: We should try to find new jobs for those who are going to be fired.

Ann: I don't see a point in getting us involved in the labour market.

John: Let me shed some light on this.

Ann: By all means.

John: Joining forces with the trade union lowers the risk of a strike.

Ann: I have to admit it's a strong argument. Sooner or later we might have to face the possibility of another strike.

---

trade union 노동조합 | **board** 경영진 | **be in a dilemma over** ~에 대해 딜레마에 빠져 있다 | **by all means** 물론, 아무렴 | **joining forces** 합세, 힘을 합침 | **lower** ~를 낮추다

Vocabulary plus

acceptable 받아들일 수 있는

aim 목적, 목표

as clear as day 명명백백한

bargaining chip 협상 카드

bottom line 핵심

bring to the negotiating table 협상의 장으로 복귀하다

bury the hatchet 화해하다

caring 배려하는, 보살피는

chair 의장을 맡다

close ties 친밀한 관계

come to a dead end 진퇴양난에 빠지다

contribute 의견을 말하다

damaging 해로운

floor 바닥

give away 거저 주다

give the green light 허가를 내주다

have strong reservations 강한 의문을 가지다

horse-trading 흥정

initiative 계획; 주도권

kick off ~를 시작하다

labour force 노동력

lay one's cards on the table 속내를 다 드러내 보이다

let time take its course 시간에 맡기다

light at the end of the tunnel 고난 끝의 광명

loyalty 충성

Not necessarily. 꼭 그렇지는 않다.

payment term 납기

pour oil on troubled waters 분쟁을 가라앉히다

prolonged 장기적인

put forward (의견 등을) 내놓다

reach a compromise 타협에 이르다

reach the goal 목표에 도달하다

redundancy payment 퇴직 수당

side effect 부작용

sweep under the carpet ~를 숨기려 들다

sweeping generalization 포괄적인 일반화

take a back seat (지위에서) 물러나다

take steps 조치를 취하다

the floor is somebody's ~ 차례이다

think out of the box 독창적으로 생각하다

threat of a strike 파업 위협

trade-off 거래

volume of supply 공급량

welcome 환영받는

willingness 기꺼이 하는 마음

win-win solution 모두에게 유리한 해결책

written proposal 제안서

Cultural tips

Did you know that ...?

A trade union (a labor union in American English) is an organization of workers who have united to achieve common goals such as protecting the integrity of its trade, improving safety standards, achieving higher pay and benefits such as health care and retirement, and better working conditions.

Scene 10 (46)   Film dialogue and vocabulary

Read the monologue. Check the list of words and phrases below.

Yeah ... Because when my fingers were broken, which was quite a complicated affair, since basically two of my knuckles were completely crushed ...

Yeah, it was bloody painful! ... Yeah, they inserted two pins or, I don't know, bits of wire to my hand to help support the joints, because otherwise ... Yeah, that's right ... So when I got the brand new smartphone and started to navigate through the menu with my fingers, it was like ... Holy shit! As if my hand was on fire! ... Unbearable, right? ... Yeah, so I may as well take this phone, which cost like half of my monthly wages, and wipe my arse with it!

Vocabulary

affair	일, 문제	menu	메뉴
knuckle	손가락 마디	Holy shit!	젠장!
crush	으스러뜨리다	be on fire	불이 나다
insert	삽입하다	unbearable	견딜 수 없는
pin	핀	cost	비용이 들다
wire	철사	monthly	매월의
joint	관절	wage(s)	임금
brand new	완전 새 것인	wipe one's arse with	쓸데없다
navigate (through)	탐색하다		

Olive Green

level **B2**

Read the dialogue between Murray (M) and Willis (W). Check the list of words and phrases below.

Olive, it would be wise to drop the gun. You still might come out of this alive. Though, I'm making no promises.

W: You recognise me?

M: Recognise you! You sad, twisted piece of turd! I've had my eye on you since I gave you that beating in the road. You've had me observed for years, but I've had you observed, too.

W: I don't believe it!

M: Really? Then why am I here? Could it be because someone you've always trusted has been on my payroll for years? It's highly probable, isn't it? The truth is I know I should have had you done in years back, but … I just took such pleasure in watching you grow.

Vocabulary				
	wise	현명한	observe	주시하다
	alive	살아 있는	be on a payroll	돈을 받다
	make a promise	약속하다	highly probable	일어날 가능성이 매우 높은
	twisted	(마음이) 비뚤어진	truth	사실, 진실
	piece of turd	양아치	do in	죽이다
	have an eye on	~를 지켜보다	take pleasure (in)	즐거움을 얻다
	road	길	grow	자라다

level B2 Scene 10 (46)

Grammar explanations

관계사절의 한정적 용법 Defining relative clauses

This is the person who recommended the film to me.
이 사람이 제게 영화를 추천해 준 사람이에요.

You are looking at the school where I learnt everything I know.
당신은 제가 알고 있는 모든 것을 배웠던 학교를 보고 있어요.

→ 한정적 용법의 관계사절은 필수적인 정보를 보여준다. 관계사절은 관계대명사와 관계부사를 통해 주절과 연결된다.

- 사람을 한정시키는 who (or that)

  Vlad is definitely the person who terrifies me most.
  Vlad는 분명 저를 가장 두렵게 만드는 사람이에요.

- 사물을 한정시키는 which (or that)

  I don't remember the name of the painting which Olive was supposed to steal.
  Olive가 훔치고자 했던 그림의 이름이 생각나지 않는군요.

- 장소를 한정시키는 where

  I like the interior of the B&B where Olive decided to stay.
  저는 Olive가 머물기로 경정한 B&B의 인테리어가 좋습니다.

- 시간을 한정시키는 when

  The story begins when Olive receives a phone call.
  그 이야기는 Olive가 전화를 받았을 때 시작되죠.

- 소유자를 한정시키는 whose

  Robert Murray is the man whose painting must be stolen.
  Robert Murray는 도난당한 것이 분명한 그림의 주인이에요.

→ 전치사 뒤의 who는 whom으로 바뀐다.

At the beginning of the story Olive doesn't know the man to whom she talks on the phone. 이야기가 시작되는 부분에서, Olive는 자신과 전화 통화를 했던 사람을 알지 못합니다.

Kirsch is the man from whom Olive is trying to escape.
Kirsch는 Olive가 벗어나려고 했던 사람입니다.

전치사를 문미에 두는 것이 더 격식 있다.

At the beginning of the story Olive doesn't know the man who she talks to on the phone. 이야기가 시작되는 부분에서, Olive는 자신과 전화 통화를 했던 사람을 알지 못합니다.

Kirsch is the man who she is trying to escape from. Kirsch는 Olive가 벗어나려고 했던 사람입니다.

→ which 혹은 whom은 관계사절에 또 다른 주어가 있을 경우 생략할 수 있다.

She is writing a story of an art thief who(m) she met personally.
→ She is writing a story of an art thief she met personally.
그녀는 그녀가 직접 만났던 미술품 도둑의 이야기를 쓰고 있습니다.

She is writing a story about an art thief who lived in this house. (생략 불가)
그녀는 이 집에 살았던 미술품 도둑에 관한 이야기를 쓰고 있습니다.

I can't recall the name of the painting which Olive intends to steal.

→ I can't recall the name of the painting Olive intends to steal.
저는 Olive가 훔치려고 했던 그림의 이름이 기억나지 않습니다.

I can't recall the name of the painting **which** is so valuable for Olive's client. (생략 불가)
저는 Olive의 고객이 소중하게 생각했던 그림의 이름이 기억나지 않습니다.

David has a gun **which** he took from the police station.
→ David has a gun he took from the police station.
David는 경찰서에서 가지고 온 총을 소지하고 있습니다.

David has a gun **which** is the property of the police station. (생략 불가)
David는 경찰서 자산인 총을 소지하고 있습니다.

관계사절의 계속적 용법 Non-defining relative clauses

→ 계속적 용법의 관계사절은 불필요하거나 부가적인 정보를 보여준다. 관계사절은 쉼표로 주절과 분리된다.

None of the characters in the film play musical instruments, **which** is a pity.
그 영화의 어떤 등장 인물도 악기를 연주하지는 않는데, 이는 안타까운 점입니다.

Remember!
계속적 용법에서는 **which / who** 대신에 **that**을 사용할 수 없다.

Olive Green, **who** speaks English with a strong American accent, is the main heroine.
Olive Green은, 강한 미국식 억양으로 영어를 하는데, 여주인공입니다.

David's mother runs a small guesthouse, **which** I like very much.
David의 어머니는 작은 게스트하우스를 운영하는데, 저는 이곳을 매우 좋아합니다.

Get something done / Have something done

→ 다른 누군가에게 어떤 것을 하도록 시킬 때 **have something done**을 사용한다.
→ **get something done**은 **have something done**보다 일상적인 표현이다.

Martin **had** the documents **stolen** from Murray's mansion. (he employed Olive to do it)
Martin은 Murray의 저택에서 문서를 훔치도록 했습니다. (그는 Olive를 고용해서 그렇게 했습니다.)

The dress Olive bought is too wide. She will **have** it **taken in**. (a dressmaker will take care of it)
Olive가 구입한 드레스는 폭이 너무 넓었습니다. 그녀는 옷을 줄이도록 할 것입니다. (재봉사가 그 일을 할 것입니다.)

Murray will **get** the stab wound **dressed** as soon as possible.
Murray는 가능한 빨리 자상에 붕대가 감기도록 할 거예요.

He **got** the painting **copied** in case of burglary or fire.
도난이나 화재를 대비해서 그는 그 그림을 복제하도록 했어요.

Communication situations

Read the following dialogues between friends. One of them is changing jobs.

So, you quit your job. That's a very brave move. Have you started looking for a new one? I'm asking because I might have an offer for you.

Dialogue 1

B: Thanks mate, but I'm not interested. I'm about to enter e-commerce.

A: Oh, are you? That's a big step. When are you going to start?

B: In about a month or so.

A: Well done! What are you going to deal with?

B: I'm going to run an online currency exchange.

A: Interesting. How'll that work?

B: It's simple. You pay some money into my account and I transfer the currency you want into yours.

A: That's clear enough. But where will you get the currency from?

B: That's the main part of the business. You go into the global online market.

A: Blimey. You're taking to it like a duck to water. I'll keep my fingers crossed for you!

---

currency exchange 환전소 | **take to something like a duck to water** (물에 들어간 오리처럼) ~에 쉽게 익숙해지다

Dialogue 2

B: And what is it? I'll be happy to consider an offer from you.

A: I'm thinking of taking my business online, you know. The only problem is that I'm used to cash and I don't trust online transactions.

B: Online business is a good idea. What would I be responsible for?

A: I'd like you to take care of the cash flow and of the whole financial part of the business.

B: I'll be happy to give you a hand.

A: Deal! So now, about the details …

cash flow 자금 흐름 | **give a hand** 도움을 주다

Dialogue 3

B: Cash is king. I know. But …

A: What do you mean?

B: Cash and the net don't go along.

A: You just watch me! I'll be a pioneer in the development of a new model of e-commerce.

B: I don't want to be a prophet of doom here but without online payment system your venture will fail.

A: Really, have some faith! That's the point! No fancy "online payments", only cash. So, are you in or out?

B: Wake up! It won't work! I know this sector.

A: We're obviously not going to see eye to eye on this. Well, let's watch the match, it's starting.

king 가장 중요한, 최고의; 왕 | **net** 인터넷 | **go along** 어울리다 | **pioneer** 선구자 | **development** 개발, 발달 | **prophet of doom** 비관론을 퍼뜨리는 사람 | **payment system** 결제 시스템 | **venture** 모험적 사업 | **Have some faith!** 믿어 봐! | **Are you in or out?** 같이 할래, 아니면 빠질래? | **see eye to eye on** 의견이 일치하다

level B2 Scene 10 (46)

Vocabulary plus

absolutely 전적으로
annual turnover 연간 매출
as needed 필요에 따라
box 상자; 네모, 칸
bureau de change 환전소
compensate 보상하다
contactless 비접촉의
contradictory 모순되는
currency trading 통화 거래
customer 손님, 고객
darts 다트
e-banking 전자금융
entrepreneur 사업가
excluded 제외되는
expense 지출
fat cat 배부른 자본가
fee 수수료
foreign currency 외화
from one's perspective ~의 관점에서
go swimmingly 순조롭게 진행되다
gran 할머니
hunch 예감

individual 개인
market research 시장 조사
missus 부인, 아내
mobile payments 모바일 결제
move 행동
not to have the slightest 전혀 모르는
pay the bills 계산하다, 지불하다
profit 이익을 얻다
profit margin 이윤 폭
quit one's job 사직하다
random characters 임의의 글자
redirect 방향을 바꾸다
shop talk (자신의) 직장에 대한 이야기
taking into account ~를 고려하여
test the waters 미리 상황을 살피다
That's a start. 이제 시작이네요.
The beginning is always the hardest. 시작이 가장 힘들다.
The next round's on you. 다음 술은 당신이 사세요.
unrealistic 비현실적인
up and running 운영 중인
What's the world coming to? 세상에나!

Cultural tips

Did you know that ...?

Darts is a form of throwing game in which small missiles are thrown at a circular dartboard fixed to a wall. Darts is a traditional pub game, commonly played in the United Kingdom, across the Commonwealth, Republic of Ireland, the United States, and elsewhere. It was first played around the 1860s in the United Kingdom.

Scene 11 (47) Film dialogue and vocabulary

Read the dialogue between Murray (M), Willis (W), Olive (O) and David (D). Check the list of words and phrases below.

In fact, I believe I deserve credit for making you the man you are now.

Credit for making me … You deluded idiot!

W: You have ruined my life! … And hers! If Beatrice hadn't been taken away from me … !

M: I don't want this name to be uttered again! It's giving me headache! We both know this has nothing to do with my wife! Admit it! What's been driving you for the past 29 years is not longing for a love lost. You just wanted to get even with me. But you'll never do it! … How does this make you feel, huh? A nightmare come true? Olive, give me the folder, let's end this sorry affair.

O: I don't have it!

M: You don't? Does he?

O: No. The folder has been misplaced.

M: Misplaced? … You mean you don't know where it is?

D: I've got it!

M: That's just … Wow! Has one more boy been turned into a man on my account?

D: Now, let me tell you how this is going to end! To start with, here's your precious folder … (…)

M: This feels familiar … you crawling in the mud in front of me, helpless and pathetic.

level B2

Vocabulary

deserve credit (for)	~대해 공로를 인정받다	sorry	한심한, 보잘것없는
deluded	착각에 빠진	misplace	잘못 두다
utter	말하다	turn into	~이 되다
give a headache	두통을 일으키다	on account (of)	~때문에
longing (for)	~에 대한 갈망	familiar	익숙한
get even (with)	~에게 대갚음하다	crawl	(엎드려) 기다
come true	이루어지다, 실현되다	helpless	무력한
folder	서류철, 폴더	pathetic	불쌍한

But this time ...

level B2 Scene 11 (47)

Grammar explanations

조동사의 수동태 Passive voice with modal verbs

➔ 문장의 주어가 중요하지 않거나 명확하지 않을 때, 조동사는 종종 수동태로 쓰인다. 이 경우 be동사를 동반한다.

Somebody should tell David the truth about Olive. ➔ David **should be told** the truth about Olive. 누군가가 Olive에 관한 진실을 David에게 말해야 해요. → David는 Olive에 관한 진실을 들어야 해요.

Or better not! They must keep him in the dark! ➔ Or better not! He **must be kept** in the dark! 어찌됐든! 그에게는 비밀로 해야 해요. → 어찌됐든! 그는 비밀을 몰라야 해요.

Cloutier **must be freed** or he will get crazy listening to Alfie.
Cloutier는 풀려나야 하는데, 그렇지 않으면 그는 Alfie의 말을 듣고 미쳐버릴 거예요.

The food David left them **will not** even **be touched**.
David가 그들에게 남긴 음식은 처음 그대로 남아 있을 거예요.

Garages such as Alfie's **should be searched** and **locked down** by the authorities.
Alfie의 것과 같은 차고는 당국에 의해 조사되고 봉쇄되어야 해요.

➔ 과거에 대해 추정할 때, 조동사는 수동태로 쓰일 수 있다.

Olive shouldn't have taken the job! Somebody could have hurt her badly. ➔ She **could have been hurt** badly.
Olive는 그 일을 맡지 말아야 해요! 누군가가 그녀를 크게 해칠 수 있었어요. → 그녀는 크게 다칠 수도 있었어요.

If she had waited a while more, they would have given her a better offer.
➔ If she had waited a while more, she **would have been given** a better offer.
그녀가 조금 더 기다렸다면 그들은 그녀에게 더 좋은 제안을 했을 수도 있어요.
→ 그녀가 조금 더 기다렸다면 그녀는 더 좋은 제안을 받았을 수도 있어요.

Olive Green

it is thought, it is not known, it was believed

➜ 정보의 출처가 명확하지 않거나 중요하지 않을 때, 수동태로 내용을 전달할 수 있다.

It is said that people watching 'Olive Green' make astounding progress in English.
Olive Green을 시청하는 사람들의 영어 실력은 놀라울 정도로 향상될 것이라고 말해집니다.

It was believed that text books and workbooks were the only way to master any language. 교재와 워크북은 언어를 마스터할 수 있는 유일한 방법이라고 생각됩니다.

위와 같은 형태로 쓰일 수 있는 동사의 예: think, report, state, claim, maintain, rumour

➜ 구어체에서는 주어가 문두에 온다.

People watching 'Olive Green' **are said to make** astounding progress in English.
Olive Green을 시청하는 사람들의 영어 실력은 놀라울 정도로 향상될 것이라고 말해집니다.

Text books and workbooks **were believed to be** the only way to master any language.
교재와 워크북은 언어를 마스터할 수 있는 유일한 방법이라고 생각됩니다.

주어 + 수동태 형식의 전달 동사 + to부정사

➜ 수동태 전달 동사는 대개 단순현재시제로 쓰인다.

We believe (now) that David is a good cop (now). ➜ David **is believed to be** a good cop.
우리는 David가 우수한 경찰이라고 믿습니다. → David는 우수한 경찰이라고 생각됩니다.

➜ 수동태 전달 동사는 과거에 발생했던 일을 전달한다.

We also think (now) that coming to Alfie's garage was a mistake (then).
➜ Coming to Alfie's garage **is thought to have been** a mistake.
또한 우리는 Alfie의 차고에 온 것이 실수였다고 생각합니다. → Alfie의 차고로 온 것은 실수라고 생각됩니다.

주어 + 수동태 형식의 전달 동사 + *to have done*

➜ 수동태 전달 동사는 현재 일어나고 있는 일을 전달한다.

We believe Olive is having a good time some place now.
➜ Olive **is believed to be having** a good time some place now.
우리는 Olive가 지금 어딘가에서 좋은 시간을 보내고 있다고 믿습니다.
→ Olive는 지금 어딘가에서 좋은 시간을 보내고 있다고 생각됩니다.

주어 + 수동태 형식의 전달 동사 + *to be doing*

level B2 Scene 11 (47)

Communication situations

Read the following dialogues. David and Jessica are discussing new technologies.

What's that noise? Mum, was that you? Are you OK?

Dialogue 1

Jessica: No. It's the third time I'm reading this manual.

David: OK. Easy. What manual?

Jessica: A manual for this blender.

David: OK. What's the problem?

Jessica: Look here. "You must place the jug onto the power base first".

David: And what is it that you don't understand here?

Jessica: Which jug do they mean? There are two in the box.

David: Either will do. You're just not supposed to turn the blender on without a jug in place, that's all.

---

blender 믹서기 | **jug** 용기 | **power base** 전원이 들어오는 본체

Dialogue 2

Jessica: Am I hopeless at technology or is it just the weather?

David: I think neither. What's wrong?

Jessica: I've been trying to register an account for this application but it doesn't work.

David: Mum, stop clicking on the "log in" button. You need to "sign up" or "create an account".

Jessica: Right ... You log into an account that you already have! Silly me!

David: OK. Let's see what comes next. They want your personal data and e-mail.

Jessica: That's easy. Look.

David: Stop! What are you doing? Don't give them your real name or date of birth!

Jessica: Why not?

David: Because it's the Internet! Somebody may misuse your data. You need to be careful.

register 등록하다 | **application** 어플리케이션 | **click** 딸깍하는 소리 | **sign up** 가입하다 | **create** 만들다 | **personal data** 개인 정보 | **date of birth** 생년월일 | **misuse** 악용하다

Dialogue 3

Jessica: The computer doesn't like me.

David: What do you mean? What's the matter? Maybe I could help?

Jessica: It shuts down every five minutes.

David: That sounds bad. Is it still on warranty?

Jessica: I don't know. I throw such things away.

David: Warranties? Seriously? You are unbelievable.

shut down (기계가) 멈추다 | **on warranty** 보증기간 이내 | **throw away** 버리다 | **unbelievable** 믿을 수 없는

Dialogue 4

Jessica: I'd like to start a blog but I don't understand the procedure.

David: A blog? OK. First, you have to find a server which hosts a public blogging platform.

Jessica: I know all that. I'm stuck on the technical side of it.

David: Well, then you need to log into your panel and install the blogging platform. It should be under "website builders".

Jessica: OK. I'm about to start. I'll find you if I need you again.

---

procedure 절차 | install 설치하다

Vocabulary plus

back up 백업하다

correct 고치다

correspond to ~에 일치하다

entry 항목

firmly 꽉

gently 부드럽게

ink roll 잉크 롤

lend a hand 도움을 주다

license 허가증

mode 방식, 모드

noise 소음

outlet 콘센트

paid 유료의

Piece of cake! 식은 죽 먹기지!

plug in 전원을 연결하다

pop-up ads 팝업 광고

press down 누르다

regularly 규칙적으로

repurchase 다시 사다

restore 회복시키다

snap into place 위치에 맞게 잘 들어가다

switch 전환하다

tutorial 사용 지침서

type plate 극판

voltage 전압

work out 처리하다

Cultural tips

Did you know that ...?

Dates are written differently in British and American English.

The most common way in British English is to write the day of the month first, then the month (starting with a capital letter) and then the year, for example: 16 September 2016 (or 16/09/2016 in short). With the exception of May and June, months can be shortened as follows: Jan, Feb, Mar, Apr, Jul, Aug, Sept, Oct, Nov, Dec.

In written American English, the month of the date comes before the day and year. For example, Independence Day in the USA is on July 4th each year. In the year 2000 the date was 4/7/2000 in British English. In American English this is written 7/4/2000.

Scene 12 (48)   Film dialogue and vocabulary

Read the dialogue between David (D) and Olive (O). Check the list of words below.

D: What address? You're dying here! You need a surgeon!
O: Brooks … is a surgeon. Sort of … Damn, it hurts! Money … the money!
D: How can you even think about that!
O: No … you don't … It's for Brooks. That wacko … ain't cheap!

bleed	피를 흘리다	wacko	미친 사람, 괴짜
surgeon	(외과) 의사		

Read Murray's monologue. Check the list of words and phrases below.

This is Murray. I'm calling about the Olive situation.

Yes, I know I told you that things are under control, but apparently ... Yes, I have retrieved it, but some of the data is missing and it may be relevant to our cooperation. I did promise you that this wouldn't put your business at risk, but since your men failed, I had to deal with it myself, didn't I? (...) I understand. Your place, tomorrow at noon. Short-term though, some steps need to be taken. We had a little gunfight. Some of the participants might still be alive. They know things about me, so can you send your men there to make sure they'll never share them? I'll make it up to you, Gennady! I will.

Vocabulary				
	be under control	잘 관리되다	short-term	단기의
	be missing	사라지다	take steps (to)	조치를 취하다
	relevant	관련 있는	gunfight	총싸움
	cooperation	협력	participant	관계자
	put at risk	~를 위험에 처하게 하다	make up to	~에게 보상을 하다
	noon	정오		

Grammar explanations

고급 간접 화법 Advanced reported speech

→ 간접 화법 문장은 시간의 흐름을 보여준다.

Murray **told** David that his mother **had run** into serious financial problems.
Murray는 David에게 자신의 어머니가 심각한 금전적인 문제를 겪고 있다고 말했어요.

→ 진행 중이거나 현 상황에 대해 말할 때는 시간의 흐름이 드러나지 않는다.

I **told** you we **have** something in common, David!
제가 당신에게 우리에게는 공통점이 있다고 말했잖아요, David!

I **said** that there **is** a lot of mess to clean.
저는 치워야 할 것들이 많다고 말했어요.

→ **say** something (to somebody) / **tell** somebody something

The security guard **said** that he had some serious problems with navigating his smartphone. 경비원은 자신의 스마트폰을 조작하는데 심각한 문제를 겪고 있다고 말했어요.

He also **told his friend** that the gadget cost half his monthly wage.
그는 또한 친구에게 그 기기의 값이 자신 월급의 절반에 해당된다고 말했어요.

→ **say**와 **tell**은 상황에 따라 **admit**과 **deny**와 같은 보다 더 적절한 동사로 대체될 수 있다.

Olive **said** that she needed to protect the people she cared for. → Olive **admitted** that she needed to protect the people she cared for.
Olive는 자신이 좋아하는 사람들을 그녀가 보호해야 한다고 말했어요. → Olive는 자신이 좋아하는 사람들을 그녀가 보호해야 한다는 점을 인정했어요.

David **said** that he wasn't working for Murray. → David **denied** working for Murray.
David는 자신이 Murray를 위해 일하지 않는다고 말했어요. → David는 Murray를 위해 일한다는 점을 부인했어요.

→ **admit, claim, complain** + that절

Sergey: Dad, but he is a mindless lunatic!
→ Sergey **complained that** Vlad **was** a mindless lunatic.
Sergey: 아빠, 하지만 그는 아무 생각이 없는 미치광이라고요! → Sergey는 Vlad가 아무 생각이 없는 미치광이라고 불평했습니다.

→ **suggest, deny, insist on** + 동명사

David: Don't you think we should talk to the police?
→ David **insisted on** talk**ing** to the police.
David: 우리가 경찰에게 말해야 한다고 생각하지 않나요? → David는 경찰에게 말하자고 주장했습니다.

→ **promise, refuse, threaten, encourage, warn** + to부정사

Vlad: I'll be after you in no time!
→ Vlad **threatened to be** after them in no time.
Vlad: 곧 너희를 뒤쫓을 것이다! → Vlad는 곧 그들을 뒤쫓겠다고 위협했습니다.

Communication situations

Read the following dialogues between the participants of a corporate meeting about financial results.

Good morning, ladies and gentlemen, and thanks for coming. As you know from the agenda, we are going to talk about last year sales result.

Dialogue 1

B: So let's start the ball rolling.

A: We have broken our presentation into 4 parts.

B: The first three depict raw data concerning our development overseas.

A: The fourth and the last one is for questions.

B: Nevertheless, feel free to stop us if you have any doubts.

A: That's all for the start. Now, let's have a look at the first slide.

---

start the ball rolling 일을 시작하다 ⁞ **break into** 나누다 ⁞ **presentation** 발표 ⁞ **depict** 묘사하다, 설명하다 ⁞ **overseas** 해외에 ⁞ **slide** 슬라이드

Dialogue 2

A: We'd like to start by showing you our share in the market.

B: Then we'll move on to the second part which is about the factors influencing our position.

A: We'd like to focus on both the internal and external factors.

B: Moving on to part three, we will propose a diagnosis and outline possible solutions for the problems presented. We'll also put forward some suggestions for further development.

A: And finally, we'll recap all the main points of the presentation.

B: Ladies and gentlemen, let's get started. When it comes to presentations, the shorter, the sweeter.

share 공유하다; 지분 | **influence** 영향을 미치다 | **internal** 내부의 | **external** 외부의 | **factor** 요인 | **diagnosis** 진단 | **outline** ~대해 간추려 말하다 | **possible** 가능성 있는 | **recap** 요약하다

Dialogue 3

B: First, we're going to talk about our forecasts made last year.

A: As you can see, we were quite optimistic.

B: Prematurely, as it turned out. But we'll come back to it later.

A: The second slide presents a percentage bar chart.

B: It compares us to our competitors.

A: Please keep this picture in mind, as we will go into more details on that later. But for now …

forecast 예측 | **prematurely** 이르게, 시기 상조로 | **percentage** 백분율 | **bar chart** 막대그래프 | **compare** 비교하다 | **keep that in mind** 그것을 명심하다 | **picture** 그림

Vocabulary plus

as a result 결과적으로
brainstorming 브레인스토밍
comment 의견
constant growth 끊임없는 발전
core 핵심
dip 하락
discussion 논의
due to ~ 때문에
end up 결국 ~이 되다
estimate 추정하다
examine 검토하다
first of all 우선
growth rate 성장률
illustrate 분명히 보여주다; 삽화를 넣다
in due order 순차적으로
in time 제때
in-house 내부의
last but not least 마지막으로 (그러나 또한 중요한)
line graph 선그래프
overlapping 중복된

overview 개요
plenty of time 충분한 시간
point out 지적하다
predict 예측하다
proceed 진행하다
process 과정
quarter 분기
recover 회복하다
refer 나타내다, 참고하다
remain steady 안정된 상태를 유지하다
represent 나타내다
sales result 매출 실적
sharp decline 급격한 하락
stagnate 침체되다
steady 꾸준한
summary 요약
underline 밑줄 긋다, 강조하다
unexpected 뜻밖의
unknown 알려지지 않은

Cultural tips

Did you know that ...?

In ordinary English speech, the twelve-hour clock is used. There are two common ways of telling the time:

1. Formal but easier way: Say the hours first and then the minutes, e.g. 7:45 – seven forty-five. For minutes 01 to 09, you can pronounce the "0" as oh, e.g. 11:06 – eleven (oh) six.

2. More popular way: Say the minutes first and then the hours. Use 'past' and the preceding hour for the minutes 01 to 30. Use "to" and the approaching hour for minutes 31 to 59, e.g. 7:15 – fifteen minutes past seven / a quarter past seven, 7:45 – fifteen minutes to eight / a quarter to eight, 5:30 – thirty minutes past five / half past five. To make it clear (where necessary) whether you mean a time before 12 o'clock noon or after, you can use 'in the morning', 'in the afternoon', 'in the evening', 'at night'. More formal expressions to indicate whether a time is before noon or after are a.m./am (also: am – ante meridiem, before noon) and p.m./pm (also: pm – post meridiem, after noon). Use these expression only with the formal way of telling the time.

Translation 해석

Scene 1 (37)

Film dialogue and vocabulary p. 8~10

U: 마틴, 브라이언 데이비슨한테 보낼 송장을 내가 어디 뒀는지 혹시 아니?
M: 놀랄 준비하세요, 삼촌!
M: 바로 이 서랍에 지난 6달간의 모든 송장이 있어요. 시간순으로 분류해 뒀죠.
U: 내가 뭐랬니? 여긴 곧 네가 운영하게 될 거야! 그럼, 점심 전에 한 군데만 더 갔다 오면 돼. 거기가 맘에 들 거야!

M: 안녕하세요? 꽃들이 예쁘네요!
M: 이 저택의 돈 많은 노인네들 식탁에 올려놓으면 멋지겠어요!
B: 이 저택의 돈 많은 노인네들은 꽃에 전혀 관심이 없어요. 겉만 번지르르하다니요.
M: 꽃을 좋아하지도 않으면서 왜 당신을 고용한 거죠?
B: 제가 재미로 하는 거예요. 진저리가 나게 지루한 곳이거든요. 베아트리스 캠벨이에요. 이 저택의 더럽게 돈 많은 노인네들의 딸이죠.

ask Beatrice out
M: 전 마틴이에요. 그렇게 지루하게 둘 순 없죠. 비인간적이잖아요. 나랑 같이… 드라이브 가는 건 어때요?
B: 드라이브요?

leave
B: 저기요, 곧 배달해줄 일이 있을 것 같은데요! 연락드려도 돼요? 아니면 바쁘세요?

Communication situations p. 12~13

Boss: 들어오세요… 오 안녕하세요, 오늘 만남에 응해 줘서 기뻐요. 앉으세요. 알다시피, 우리는 당신의 360도 평가에 대해 이야기할 거예요. 전반적으로, 저희는 당신의 작년 성과에 만족하고 있어요. 또한 당신은 동료들로부터 긍정적인 평가도 받았어요. 잘했어요. 하지만 세부적인 내용을 말하기에 앞서 당신의 말을 먼저 듣고 싶어요. 지난 12개월이 당신에게도 만족스러웠나요?

Dialogue 1
Employee: 네, 저는 제 성과에 만족해요. 하지만 이야기하고 싶은 것들이 몇 가지 있어요.

Boss: 예를 들면요?

Employee: 업무량이 줄었으면 좋겠어요.

Boss: 그렇군요. 하지만 당신은 입사할 때 업무 범위에 대해 들었잖아요.

Employee: 정확히는 아니었죠.

Boss: 어째서죠?

Employee: 계획된 것보다 더 많은 프로젝트가 시작되었어요. 그리고 저는 현재 일에 파묻혀 지내고 있고요.

Boss: 오, 그렇군요. 음, 당신은 그것을 도전으로 받아들여야 해요.

Employee: 이런 식의 도전은 제 근로 의욕을 꺾어놓아요.

Boss: 음, 그런 이야기를 들으니 유감이군요.

Dialogue 2

Employee: 목표를 달성해서 기뻐요. 하지만 몇 가지는 완벽하지 못했어요.

Boss: 예를 들면요?

Employee: 인센티브 프로그램은 적용되지 않더군요.

Boss: 무슨 말인가요?

Employee: 음, 휴일 근무 수당도 없고, 병가 수당도 없고, 퇴직 연금도 없잖아요.

Boss: 꼭 그렇지는 않아요. 회사에서 더 높은 직위에 오르면 모두 받게 되죠. 하지만 그렇게 되기 위해서는 시간이 걸리고 노고와 헌신이 필요하죠.

Employee: 헌신이라 함은 무엇을 의미하나요? 자정에 전화를 받는 것이요?

Boss: 알겠지만 그것이 결정적인 요인은 아니에요.

Dialogue 3

Employee: 네, 그랬어요. 주로 저의 뛰어난 결과 때문이었죠.

Boss: 정말 그래요. 당신의 결과는 인상적이었어요.

Employee: 인정해 주시다니 기쁘군요.

Boss: 당신의 우리 팀의 소중한 팀원이에요. 그럼에도 불구하고, 항상 개선의 여지는 있을 거예요.

Employee: 음, 성과 차원에서 보자면, 시간이 돈이죠.

Boss: 동의해요. 계속해 보세요.

Employee: 저는 출퇴근에 너무 많은 시간을 뺏기고 있어요.

Boss: 어떤 해결 방안을 제시하겠어요?

Employee: 일주일에 두 번은 재택 근무를 하고 싶어요.

Boss: 오, 안타깝지만 그건 당신 직책에서는 논의가 불가능한 문제예요.

Scene 2 (38)

Film dialogue and vocabulary p. 16~17

B: 최고급 와인을 가져왔어요. 풍미가 최고죠. 해산물과 고급 치즈와도 궁합이 완벽해요.
M: 잘됐네요. 마침 치즈 크래커가 있거든요.
B: 부모님은요? 당신 학비를 안 보태주세요?
M: 돈이 손에 들어오는 족족 술로 날려버리죠! 엉망진창이라고 할 수 있어요.
B: 우리 부모님들보단 나을 걸요. 아빠는 지역 여우 사냥 협회 회장이고 엄마는… 유일한 관심사가 얼굴에 주름 없애는 거예요. 런던 리츠 호텔에서 친구들 만날 때 멋져 보여야 하니까요.
M: 제정신이 아니시네요! 하지만 딸은 나름 괜찮게 키운 것 같은데요. 무난하게 예쁘고, 너무 멍청하지도 않고, 약간 특이하기 하지만요.
B: 특이하다고요?
M: 네, 하지만 그런 점이 좋아요.

insist

M: 겁낼 거 없어요!
B: 날 또 만나려면 한 가지 명심할 게 있어요. 절대 강요하지 말아요!
M: 안 할게요! 절대요! 그런데… 다음에 분위기가 더 무르익으면요?

apologize

M: 미안해요. 내가 너무 지나쳤어요!
B: 나쁘진 않았어요. 하지만 캠벨 저택에서는 이렇게 안 해요.
M: 캠벨 저택에서는 어떻게 하는데요?
B: 계속 만나다 보면 알게 될 거예요!

Communication situations p. 20~21

Host: 말볼리오 교수님, 셰익스피어의 생애에 관해 멋진 강연을 해 주셔서 감사합니다. 교수님께서 밝혀내신 몇 가지 사항들은 정말 놀라워 보입니다. 잠시 시간을 내셔서 저희가 청중들로부터 받은 몇 가지 질문에 대해 답을 해 주실 수 있으신가요?

Dialogue 1

Professor: 물론이에요, 어떤 질문이라도 기꺼이 답을 해 드릴게요.
Host: 한 가지 질문은 항상 논란을 일으키는 것입니다. 셰익스피어가 혼자서 모든 희곡을 썼나요?
Professor: 아마 그의 것이라고 알려진 작품에서 그가 유일한 작가는 아니었을 거예요.
Host: 그렇다면, 작가들로 구성된 팀이 있었나요, 아니면 한 명의 공동 작가가 있었나요?

Professor: 희곡에 따라 다르다고 말씀을 드리고 싶군요.

Host: 어떻게 그처럼 확신하실 수 있나요?

Professor: 그는 결코 자신의 경험이 아닌 경험에 대해 생생하게 묘사를 하고 있어요. 예를 들면 유럽 여행과 같은 것이요.

Host: 그것의 논거는 무엇이죠? 톨킨이 인간계에 가 본적이 없기 때문에 그가 '반지의 제왕'을 쓴 것도 의심해 볼 수 있다는 건가요? 어쨌든…

Dialogue 2

Professor: 최선을 다해서 대답해 드릴께요.

Host: 좋습니다. 첫 번째 지적은 셰익스피어의 사적인 생활과 관련된 것입니다.

Professor: 놀랍지 않군요. 이 부분은 항상 많은 관심을 끄니까요.

Host: 그의 성적 취향은 어땠나요? 그가 결혼한 것은 알려져 있지만 그것이 위장용이었나요?

Professor: 그 문제는 그것보다 훨씬 더 복잡한 문제예요.

Host: 무슨 말씀이시죠, 교수님?

Professor: 그의 문학 작품에서 발견된 흔적들은 셰익스피어가 사실 여성이었다는 점을 암시하는 것처럼 보이기도 해요.

Host: 하지만 그것은 그의 작품을 오역하거나 – 혹은 확대 해석한 것이 아닐까요?

Professor: 물론 그런 위험성은 있어요. 하지만 우리는 저명한 연구가들에 관해 이야기하고 있어요.

Host: 알겠습니다. 이제 소네트에 대해 이야기하죠. 많은 사람들의 눈에 소네트의 저자 또한 큰 논란거리입니다.

Dialogue 3

Professor: 음, 그가 결혼을 했다는 것과 그에게 아이들이 있었다는 것은 알려져 있죠.

Host: 물론 그렇지만 그의 성적 취향은 여러 차례 논란이 되어 왔습니다, 그렇지 않나요?

Professor: 그의 성적 취향은 빙산의 일각일 뿐이에요.

Host: 무슨 말씀이시죠, 교수님?

Professor: 한 이론에 따르면 "셰익스피어"는 극작가이자 시인인 크리스토퍼 말로의 또 다른 신분이었어요.

Host: 잠시만요, 뭐라고요? 몇몇 연구가들이 셰익스피어의 존재 자체를 의심하고 있다는 말씀이신가요? 세상에…

Scene 3 (39)

Film dialogue and vocabulary   p. 24~25

F: 트럭 운전사랑 동거하는 건 절대 안 돼!

B: 훨씬 큰 야망이 있는 사람이에요! 아주 똑똑해요!

M: 17살짜리를 유혹해서 세뇌할 만큼 똑똑한 거지?

F: 네 엄마가 하려는 말은 네 남자 친구가 네가 생각하는 것과는 다른 목적이 있다는 거야!

B: 무슨 말씀이세요?

F: 얘야, 동거를 시작하자마자, 어디서 살게 될진 모르겠다만, 그는 널 임신시킬 거야. 내년 겨울이면 너는 우리 전 재산을 상속받을 아이를 낳게 되겠지. 아이의 아버지로서, 그는 그 돈의 상당 부분을 차지하게 될 거야!

B: 어떻게 그런 끔찍한 생각을 할 수 있어요?

M: 세상이 그렇단다. 사기꾼, 도둑, 건달들! 우리 계급의 사람들은 항상 위협당한단다!

F: 베아트리스, 넌 아직 법적 성인이 아니야! 그러니까 동거는커녕 교제도 허락 못 해. 몇 달 후에는… 마음대로 해!

B: 얘기 끝나셨어요?

F: 아니, 아직! 엄마와 같이 한동안 여행 좀 다녀와라.

M: 그래! 네가 우릴 버리기 전에, 몇 달 동안 널 독차지해야겠어.

B: 그래서 제가 18살이 되기까지 반년 동안 마틴에 대한 마음을 돌려놓겠다는 거군요.

F: 서로 진정으로 사랑한다면 반년이 무슨 문제가 되겠니?

> object

B: 안 갈 거예요! 마틴과 절 갈라놓을 순 없어요!

F: 그래? 생각 좀 해보자! 미성년자한테 술을 마시게 하고 그 친구가 우리 몰래 이 집에 온 적도 있겠지? 그때 도둑맞은 게 좀 있을 거야. 조사 좀 해봐야겠어, 안 그래?

B: 알았어요! 하지만 돌아오고 나면 다시는 절 못 볼 줄 아세요!

> agree

B: 네, 안 될 것 없죠! 하지만 6개월 후에도 제 감정은 변하지 않을 거예요!

Communication situations   p. 28~30

Clerk: 좋은 아침입니다. 무엇을 도와 드릴까요?

> Dialogue 1

Client: 편지를 부치고 싶어요.

Clerk: 국내로요, 아니면 해외로요?

Client: 해외인데, 항공 우편으로 부치고 싶어요.

Clerk: 어떤 서비스로 부치고 싶으신가요?

Client: 어떤 서비스를 이용할 수 있죠?

Clerk: 국제 표준, 국제 등기, 행방조회, 행방조회가 가능한 국제 등기 서비스가 있습니다.

Client: 국제 표준과 행방조회가 가능한 국제 등기 서비스의 차이는 무엇인가요?

Clerk: 행방조회가 가능한 국제 등기 서비스를 통해서는 우선적인 취급을 받을 수 있고 행방조회가 가능하며 서명을 해야 배송이 완료될 뿐만 아니라 온라인을 통한 배송 확인도 가능합니다. 이러한 혜택들은 국제 표준 서비스에서 이용이 불가능한 것들이죠.

Client: 너무 많군요. 그냥 편지일 뿐이라서요.

Clerk: 그러세요. 문제 없습니다.

Dialogue 2

Client: 이 소포를 부치고 싶어요.

Clerk: 어떻게 보내시고 싶으신가요? 로열 메일로요, 아니면 특급 서비스로요?

Client: 특급 서비스는 어떻게 되나요?

Clerk: 일반적으로 다음 날 소포가 배달됩니다. 선택하신 서비스 유형에 따라 오전 9시, 10시, 오전 중, 혹은 24시간 이내에 배달되죠. 요금은 물론 소포의 무게와 선택하신 옵션에 따라 달라집니다.

Client: 배송이 보장되나요?

Clerk: '익스프레스48'에서만요. 하지만, 모든 유형의 특급 서비스에서는 소포의 행방조회가 가능하며 배송 2분 내에 온라인 배송 확인 서명 서비스가 가능합니다.

Client: 그러면 '퍼스트 클래스 사인드 포'와 '익스프레스48'의 차이점은 무엇인가요?

Clerk: 소포의 크기와 무게입니다.

Client: 설명해 주셔서 고마워요. 생각해 보니 로열 메일로 해야 할 것 같아요.

Clerk: 문제 없습니다.

Dialogue 3

Client: 편지를 부치고 싶어요.

Clerk: 국내로요, 아니면 해외로요?

Client: 스코틀랜드로 보내는 거예요.

Clerk: 음, 스코틀랜드면 영국 내군요. 맞습니다, 국내네요.

Client: 그래요. 얼마인가요?

Clerk: '퍼스트 클래스'인가요, 아니면 '세컨드 클래스'인가요?

Client: '퍼스트 클래스'와 '세컨드 클래스'의 차이가 무엇이죠?

Clerk: '퍼스트 클래스' 배송은 토요일을 포함해서 그 다음 평일 날 배달이 되고, '세컨드 클래스'는 평일 기준으로 2–3일 내에 배송이 됩니다. 그리고 물론 가격도 다르고요.

Client: 그렇군요. '세컨드 클래스'로 해 주세요.

Dialogue 4

Client: 이 소포를 부치고 싶어요.

Clerk: 어떻게 보내시고 싶으신가요? 로열 메일로요, 아니면 특급 서비스로요?

Client: 특급 서비스로 해 주세요.

Clerk: 좋습니다. 어떤 옵션을 선택하시겠어요?

Client: '익스프레스9'로 해 주세요.

Clerk: 좋습니다. 소포는 오전 9시까지 배달될 것입니다.

Dialogue 5

Client: 이 소포를 부치고 싶어요.

Clerk: 어떻게 보내시고 싶으신가요? 로열 메일로요, 아니면 특급 서비스로요?

Client: 로열 메일로 해 주세요.

Clerk: '퍼스트 클래스'로요, 아니면 '세컨드 클래스'로요?

Client: '퍼스트 클래스'로요.

Clerk: 1kg까지이고 3.20파운드입니다.

Client: 그렇군요. '세컨드 클래스'로 해 주세요.

Scene 4 (40)

Film dialogue and vocabulary p. 32~33

M: 왜 그러세요?

M: 캠벨가에 따르면 12월 7일에 스티븐과 소피 캠벨의 영애, 베아트리스 캠벨과 결혼하는 로버트 머리는 나이 26세, 매켄지 로펌의 신임 변호사로… 이게 다 무슨 헛소리예요? 무슨 뜻이죠? 베아트리스가 떠나기 전에 며칠 동안 얘기했어요. "이따위 여행으로 바뀌는 건 없어요! 부모님이 생각해 낸 한심한 계략이에요! 제발 기다려 줘요!" 그런데 이제 결혼한다고요? 변호사하고요? 이 자식은 대체 누군데요?

U: 마틴, 둘이 사귈 때는 이런 얘기 꺼내고 싶지 않았지만 현실적으로 말하면…

M: 뭐요? 현실적으로 말하면, 나 같은 놈하고는 엮이면 안 된다고요? 돈도 없고 배우지도 못했고 쓸모없는 가난한 부모 밑에서 자란 놈요? 그딴 건 안 따지는 사람이에요!

U: 그딴 걸 안 따진 건 네가 곁에 있을 때나 그랬지! 시간을 갖고 보니까, 정신이 든 거겠지…

M: 그리고 잘난 변호사한테 빠진 거죠! 믿을 수가 없어요!

U: 안 돼, 마틴! 안 돼! 소용없어!

let Martin go
제발! 더는 일을 어렵게 만들지 마!

stop Martin
보내 줘! 달라지는 건 없어!

Communication situations p. 36~37

Interviewer: 자, 퍼즐 씨, 당신은 초자연적인 현상을 전문적으로 다룹니다. 그러한 주제에 대해 다큐멘터리도 만드셨고 책도 쓰셨죠.

Dialogue 1

Mr Puzzle: 대체적으로 말하면, 그렇습니다.

Interviewer: 9시에 출근해서 5시에 퇴근하는 전형적인 직업은 아니라는 점은 인정하시겠군요. 다루시는 일에 대해 대략적으로 알려 주실 수 있으신가요?

Mr Puzzle: 저는 불가능한 일을 하려고 노력합니다: 인간이 이해할 수 있는 범위를 넘어서는 것을 설명하는 것이죠.

Interviewer: 그렇다면, 기본적으로 사람들이 듣고 싶어하는 것을 이야기하시나요?

Mr Puzzle: 물론 그렇지 않습니다. 저는 사람들이 알 수 없는 현상을 받아드리고 그것과 함께 지낼 수 있도록 도움을 줍니다.

Interviewer: 그들이 이처럼 얼토당토 않는 것을 실제로 구매하나요? 그만 좀 하시죠.

Mr Puzzle: 무엇이 두려우신가요? 특이한 무언가를 경험해 본 적이 없으세요?

Interviewer: 비공개를 전제로 말씀드리면, 당신 말이 맞아요, 저는 두려워요. 당신이 의학적으로 제정신이 아닌 것 같아서요. 하지만, 인터뷰를 다시 해 봅시다.

Dialogue 2

Interviewer: 그러면, 솔직히 말해서 – 당신은 도대체 누구인가요?

Mr Puzzle: 저는 다른 모든 사람들이 귀를 닫고 있을 때 들을 수 있고 믿을 수 있는 사람입니다.

Interviewer: 그렇다면, 기본적으로 사람들이 듣고 싶어하는 것을 이야기하시나요?

Mr Puzzle: 아니오, 저는 제 일에 과학적인 방법과 도구를 사용합니다.

Interviewer: 추를 말씀하시는 건가요?

Mr Puzzle: 왜 빈정대시죠? 저나 제 고객들을 무시하실 필요는 없을 텐데요.

Interviewer: 좋습니다. 사과할게요. 당신의 직업이 너무 특이해서 그래요.

Dialogue 3

Mr Puzzle: 저는 과학이 설명하지 못하는 온갖 종류의 초자연적인 현상들을 조사합니다.

Interviewer: 말이 나왔으니 하는 말인데, 당신의 '초자연적인 세계'라는 제목의 최신 책에서 당신은 정말로 끔찍한 사건들을 설명하고 있잖아요. 이제 그중 일부에 대해 이야기해 봅시다.

Mr Puzzle: 정확히 무엇에 대해 이야기하고 싶으신 건가요? UFO요? 신화와 전설? 신비동물학?

Interviewer: 그 모두에 대해 간략히 말씀해 주실 수 있으신가요?

Mr Puzzle: 그건 불가능해요! 그것은 여러 가지 복잡한 문제들을 아우르는, 범위가 매우 넓은 분야죠.

Interviewer: 무슨 말씀인지 알겠습니다. 하루 종일 해도 극히 일부만 다루게 되겠군요. 정말 환상적인 삶을 살고 계시네요!

Scene 5 (41)

Film dialogue and vocabulary p. 40~41

R: 당신이 마틴인가 보군.

R: 진정해! 베아트리스가 곤란해하잖아! (…) 날 칠 생각은 하지도 말았어야지. 그 아래가 좋은가 봐! 진흙탕 속 말이야. 그 자세에 아주 익숙한 것 같은데. 사실, 그게 문제의 근원이지, 안 그래? 신분 상승에 대한 욕망… 하지만 베아트리스를 이용할 생각은 마!

B: 그만해요! 그냥 두세요!

M: 무슨 일이 있었던 거야? 떠나 있는 동안 부모님이 무슨 짓을 한 거지? 말해 봐!

B: 나 임신했어.

R: 그래, 마틴. 우린 아기를 낳을 거야! 내가 알기로는 둘 사이가 잠깐 뜨거웠던 것 같은데 똑바로 알아 둬. 다 끝났어! 베아트리스와 난 곧 결혼할 거고 난 아기에게 최상의 환경을 만들어줄 거야. 네 능력으론 불가능한 거지. 안 그래?

M: 베아트리스, 제발! 사실일 리가 없잖아!

Communication situations p. 44~45

A: 친구야 안녕, 늦어서 미안해. 알다시피 어디에나 애들, 애들, 애들이 있잖아. 오, 이미 애플 파이를 시켰구나. 현명한 걸; 여기가 시내에서 애플 파이를 최고로 잘하는 곳이지. 어쨌든, 수지, 클라라, 제시는 어디에 있니?

Dialogue 1

B: 안녕. 못 들었어?

A: 뭘 들어?

B: 수지와 존이 헤어졌어.

A: 오, 안타까운 소식이네.

B: 그리고 그건 내 잘못이야.

A: 이런, 그렇게 말하지 마. 분명 네 잘못은 아닐 거야.

B: 하지만 사실인걸. 내가 그처럼 참견하지 말았어야 했는데.

A: 무슨 말이니?

B: 내가 둘 모두를 현장에서 목격했어.

A: 뭐라고?

B: 둘 다 낯선 사람과 키스를 하고 있는 것을 보았거든.

A: 오, 난장판이군! 그래서 지금은?

B: 그들의 이혼 소송이 진행 중이야.

A: 벌써? 결혼 상담 같은 것을 받아봤어야 했는데. 유감이네.

Dialogue 2

B: 클라라는 아이들과 함께 있어야 한데.

A: 음, 나한테도 아이들이 있지만 나는 왔잖아.

B: 음, 그녀는 사고 이후에 죄책감을 느껴서 아이들과 더 많은 시간을 보내고 싶어하더라고.

A: 사고? "사고"에 대해서는 들어본 적이 없어. 무슨 일이 있었는데?

B: 아이들을 학교에 데려다 주다가 자동차 충돌 사고를 겪었지.

A: 오 이런! 무사하니?

B: 신체적으로는 그렇지만 누군가가 차를 언급하면 아직도 아이들이 불안해 해.
A: 아직 정신적인 충격을 겪고 있구나. 안 됐지만, 회복될 때까지 시간이 좀 걸릴 거야.

> Dialogue 3

B: 클라라는 인도로 떠났어.
A: 인도로? 왜?
B: 불교 신자가 되기 위해서.
A: 무슨 말이야?
B: 음, 그녀는 3년 전에 남자를 만났어.
A: 그 운 좋은 남자는 누구니?
B: 그녀의 요가 선생님이었지.
A: 오 그래, 눈치를 챘어야 했는데.

Scene 6 (42)

Film dialogue and vocabulary   p. 48~49

M: 여보세요?
U: 잘 있었니? 나다. 들었니?
M: 들었어요. 머리 짓이에요! 그동안 계획했던 일을 실행한 거죠! 얼마나 사악한 인간인지 진작 알아봐야 했어요. 그녀를 구하기 위해 더 노력해야 했어요!
U: 무슨 말을 하는 거니? 대체… 뭘 의심하는 거냐?
M: 의심요? 틀림없어요. 로버트 머리가 베아트리스의 부모님을 살해한 거예요. 이제 그가 그녀의 재산을 갈취하는 걸 막을 사람이 없어요. 야금야금, 법망을 피해가며…
U: 증거가 없잖니! 그리고 이런 말 하긴 미안하지만 베아트리스가 떠났을 때 정신을 놓고 다녔잖니. 네가 돌아와 주면 좋겠구나. 내가 자립할 수 있도록 도와줄게.
M: 말씀은 고맙지만 전 괜찮아요. 밤 근무하고 낮에 공부하면서 바쁘게 살고 있어요.
U: 잘 극복하고 있다니 다행이구나. 그런데… 돈이 필요하면, 말만 해.
M: 필요해요. 하지만 삼촌이 줄 수 있는 돈이 아니에요. 머리 같은 인간을 상대하려면, 엄청난 자금과 수단이 필요하죠. 둘 다 구하겠지만, 시간이 좀 걸릴 거예요.
U: 마틴, 그게 정상은 아닌 것 같구나. 내가 런던으로 가는 게 좋겠다. 만나서 얘기하자.
M: 그러실 필요 없어요!

> offer help

U: 내가 도와줄게, 마틴.
M: 삼촌 도움은 필요 없어요. 사실 누구의 도움도 필요 없어요. 다시는 전화하지 마세요, 아셨죠?

> persuade

U: 정신이 나간 게냐? 여자 때문에? 정신 차리고 얼른 돌아와! 몇 년 뒤면, 내 사업을 물려받을 수 있어.

M: 그렇게 말해주셔서 고마워요. 지금까지 베풀어주신 것도 다요. 만약에… 그게… 안녕히 계세요!

Communication situations p. 52~53

Ex-wife: 이건 공정하지 못해. 그 오랜 시간들! 나는 취미와 일, 그리고, 음 – 내 자신을 희생했는데, 무엇을 위한 것이었지?

Dialogue 1

Friend: 나도 알지만, 진정해, 스스로에게 상처만 줄 뿐이야.

Ex-wife: 그럴 수가 없어, 내게는 정말로 충격이었다고! 우리는 지금까지… 미안 – 우리는 전에 – 25년을 함께 살았지만 내 결혼 생활은 10분간의 이혼 재판으로 끝이 났어.

Friend: 이번 일을 새로운 삶을 위한 기회라고 받아들여.

Ex-wife: 하지만 나는 기존 삶을 좋아했어. 사랑했지. 나는 행복했고.

Friend: 하지만 그는 분명 그렇지 않았을걸. 어찌됐든, 뒤를 돌아보는 것은 소용 없는 일이야.

Ex-wife: 내가 과거를 마주할 수도 없고 미래를 바라볼 수도 없는 때에 너는 어떻게 그처럼 잔인한 말을 할 수가 있니?

Friend: 단지 네 결혼 생활이 자연스럽게 끝난 것뿐이야. 이제 다음으로 넘어갈 때라고.

Ex-wife: 아마 그럴지도… 하지만 다음이 뭔데? 이제 어떻게 하지? 나는 산산조각이 났어.

Dialogue 2

Friend: 때때로 인생은 정말로 불공정할 수 있어.

Widow: 때때로라고 했니? 인생은 항상 불공정해!

Friend: 나도 알아. 지금이 네게는 정말로 힘든 시기임에 틀림없어.

Widow: 그래, 맞아.

Friend: 물어봐서 미안한데, 상실감 때문이니, 아니면 공개된 유언장 때문이니?

Widow: 그는 수 개월 동안 병상에 있었어. 나를 화나게 만든 건 바로 유언장이야. 그가 15년 전에 작성을 했더라고.

Friend: 이제 이해가 갈 것 같은데…

Widow: 그래. 그들이 몇 년 동안 결혼한 상태가 아니었음에도 불구하고 그 여자가 상속자 중 한 명이지.

Friend: 하지만 내가 알기로는 현재 배우자로부터 상속권을 박탈할 수는 없을걸.

Widow: 나도 알지만, 그래도 그렇지! 말도 안 된다고! 그는 그에 대해 조치를 해 놓았어야만 해, 본인의 10년 전 문제를 나보고 처리하도록 놔둬서는 안 되지.

Dialogue 3

Friend: 나도 알아. 지금이 네게는 정말로 힘든 시기임에 틀림없어.

Widow: 그래, 맞아.

Friend: 그는 훌륭한 사람이었어. 그리고 너는 지극한 사랑으로 그를 돌보았잖아!

Widow: 하지만 그렇게 오랜 세월을 같이 보낸 후에 그가 나한테 남긴 것은 아무것도 없어.

Friend: 지금이 그의 유언장에 대해 이야기할 때인지는 잘 모르겠는데.

Widow: 그러면 그 시간이 언제가 되어야 맞는 거니? 먼 친척들이 모두 그의 재산을 가지고 떠난 다음이니?

Friend: 그러지 마, 그에게는 상속인을 지명할 권리가 있었어.

Widow: 하지만 그의 건강이 나빠지고 있던 시기에 그들은 도대체 어디에 있었지? 그들 다수가 피 빨아 먹는 존재들이야.

Scene 7 (43)

Film dialogue and vocabulary p. 56~57

M: 저기요, 괜찮으세요? 도와드릴까요?

M: 어디 아픈 거예요? 구급차를 부를까요?

O: 괜찮아요.

M: 무슨 약 드시는 거 있어요? 누군가가 약물을 주입한 거 같은데요!

O: 아니라고는 못 하죠!

M: 강도를 만난 거예요? 아니면 추행당했어요? 그렇다면 경찰에 신고하셔야 해요!

O: 전 그런 일을 당해도 싸요!

M: 그런 말이 어딨어요! 자책하시면 안 돼요… 놈들이 그런 건데요!

O: 네? 아뇨! 추행당한 게 아니에요. 저기요, 도와주시려는 건 고맙지만 전 괜찮아요! 어떻게 할지 혼자 생각할 시간이 필요할 뿐이에요. (…) 잠깐만요! 좀 어지러워요. 혹시 근처에 차 세워두셨어요? 병원에 가야 할 것 같아요. 이런! 내 지갑! 벤치 밑에 떨어트렸나 봐요. 돌아가서…

M: 여기 있어요! 내가 가서 가져올게요, 알았죠? 걱정하지 마요! 금방 올게요!

Communication situations p. 60~61

Employee: 안녕하세요, 좋은 아침입니다. 앉으세요. 어떻게 도와 드릴까요?

Dialogue 1

Tenant: 안녕하세요, 욕실에 문제가 있어서요.

Employee: 그러시군요. 샤워기에 관한 건가요, 욕조에 관한 건가요, 아니면 변기에 관한 건가요?

Tenant: 빌어먹을 욕조요.

Employee: 그렇군요. 문제를 설명해 주실 수 있으신가요?

Tenant: 배수관이 막힌 것 같아요.

Employee: 오, 그런 경우라면 배수관을 분해해야 해요.

Tenant: 배관공이 몇 시에 방문할 수 있을까요?

Employee: 괜찮으시다면 내일 가능합니다.

Dialogue 2

Tenant: 시설 관리자와 이야기를 하고 싶어요.

Employee: 지금 시설 관리자 사무실에 계세요. 문제가 생긴 경우라면 이곳 모두가 도움을 드릴 수 있죠. 그러면, 문제가 있으신가요?

Tenant: 아래층 이웃에게로 누수가 되는 것 같아요.

Employee: 오 이런… 보험을 들으셨나요?

Tenant: 저는 아니지만 이웃이 들었어요.

Employee: 좋습니다. 이번은 이웃 분께서 운이 좋으시네요.

Tenant: 무슨 말씀이시죠?

Employee: 음, 십중팔구 보험이 손해에 대한 보상을 해 주겠지만, 그 후에는 보험 회사가 비용을 충당하기 위해 비용 청구를 할 거예요.

Tenant: 그러면 결국에는 저한테 오겠군요.

Employee: 안타깝지만 그렇습니다.

Dialogue 3

Tenant: 오전에 정전이 되었는데 그 때 이후로 전기가 들어오지 않고 있어요.

Employee: 이상하군요. 정전에 대한 소식은 받지 못했거든요. 그리고 다른 입주자들로부터 그에 관한 보고도 받은 적이 없어요. 요금을 지불하신 것은 확실한가요?

Tenant: 다시 말씀해 주실래요?

Employee: 음, 때때로 요금을 지불해야 한다는 걸 잊으시는 분들이 계세요. 그래서 제가 묻고 있는 것이고요.

Tenant: 네, 물론 냈어요.

Employee: 좋습니다. 전기 기사와 방문 약속을 잡아볼게요.

Tenant: 하지만 제가 이틀 동안 집을 비울 것이라서 집에는 아무도 없을 텐데요.

Employee: 걱정하지 마세요. 저희에게 열쇠를 맡겨 두시면 돌아오실 때 수리가 되어 있을 거예요.

Tenant: 누군가가 찾아온다면 제가 집에 있고 싶어요.

Employee: 알겠습니다, 그런 경우라면 방문 가능 시간과 관련된 이 양식을 채워 주시면 저희가 수리 기사와 일정을 맞춰볼게요.

Scene 8 (44)

Film dialogue and vocabulary   p. 64~65

O: 데이비드, 또 나예요.

O: 전화를 안 받으니까 어디 있는지 모르겠지만… 왠지 멀리 있지 않을 것 같네요. 저기요, 그 서류들이 꼭 있어야 해요. 이거 하나는 이해해줘요. 내가 진작 말했더라면, 이렇게 되진 않았겠지만, 어쩌겠어요? 제가 사람을 못 믿는데요. 그건 그거고! 오늘 저녁에 있을 거래는… 돈 때문에 하는 게 아니에요! 정말이에요. 이번 일에 날 고용한 사람이 나에 대해 철저하게 조사를 했어요. 내 가족을 해칠 수 있는 위치에 있어요. 우리 엄마요. 진짜로 해칠 거예요. 그럴지도 몰라요. 다 엉망이에요. 인정해요. 그 사람과 머리 사이의 역겨운 게임에 제가 억지로 개입된 거예요. 이런 일에 끌어들여서 정말 미안해요.
이렇게 될 줄 몇 주 전에 알았다면, 올드 베리의 다른 숙소를 택했을 거예요. 달리 갈 만한 숙소도 없었겠지만요. 의뢰인과 연락이 닿았어요. 한 시간 뒤에 만날 거예요. 나한테 서류가 없기 때문에, 떠오르는 해결 방법은 하나뿐이에요! 아주 위험한 방법이죠. 내가 질색하는 방법이에요. 암튼, 거기 주소를 문자로 남길게요. 당신이 서류를 가져온다면, 혹시 모르죠… 우리 둘이 평범한 데이트를 할 수 있을지도요. 당신이 오지 않더라도… 원망하지는 않을게요.

O: 안녕, 데이비드.

Communication situations   p. 68~69

A: 안녕, 내가 다시 전화했어. 미안하게도 오전에는 통화를 할 수 없었거든. 매우 들떠 있는 것 같이 들리던데. 무슨 일이니?

Dialogue 1

B: 음, 나 승진했어. 경영진으로 올라갔지.
A: 축하해! 그것이 바로 네가 꿈꾸던 것 아니었니?
B: 맞아, 드디어 해냈어. 그리고 몇 가지 변화가 있을 거야.
A: 분명 있겠지. 나한테 비밀 좀 알려 줄래?
B: 좋아. 나는 불필요한 관행을 줄이고 일일 업무의 효율성을 높일 거야.
A: 벌써 거물이 된 것 같구나.
B: 그렇게 될 것이기 때문에 너도 익숙해지는 것이 좋을 거야.
A: 지금 농담하는 중이라고 말해 줄래…
B: 음, 사람들이 일을 더 잘 하도록 만들 수 있다면 서로에게 이익이 되겠지.
A: …직원들과 회사에게.
B: 그래, 바로 그거야!
A: 오 세상에, 생각이 완전히 바뀌었구나!

Dialogue 2

B: 이 얘기를 누군가에게 하게 되다니 너무 신이 난다.
A: 좋아. 듣고 있어.
B: 내가 호주에서 인턴 생활을 하게 되었어!
A: 그것이 좋은 소식이라고 생각하는 거니?
B: 물론이지! 벌써 성공한 것 같은 기분이 드는걸!

A: 그래. 그렇다면 축하해. 네가 왜 뽑힌 것 같아?

B: 음, 취업 의지가 그다지 높지 않았다면 그처럼 긍정적인 결과는 얻지 못했을 거야.

A: 오 그래, 네 태도가 분명 이유 중 하나겠지.

B: 따로 하고 싶은 말이 있니?

A: 그 인턴쉽과 그곳 근무 조건에 대해서는 몇 가지 소문이 돌고 있어. 인턴쉽에 참가하는데 그처럼 열성인 사람은 너밖에 없다는 점이 걱정스러워.

Dialogue 3

B: 회사에서 최악의 시나리오가 실현되었어.

A: 내가 맞춰 볼게. 구조조정이 시작되려고 하는구나.

B: 맞아, 그리고 나는 최종 결정을 내려야 할 것 같아.

A: 브라보! 최종 결정이 뭐니?

B: 바로 지금이 내 사업을 시작해야 할 때인 것 같아.

A: 그것이 최선의 해결책이라고 확신해?

B: 지금 시도하지 않으면 두 번째 기회는 없을 지도 몰라.

A: 그에 대해서는 네 말이 분명 맞는 것 같은데.

B: 그리고 사업이 잘 되지 않으면 다른 일자리를 찾아볼 거야.

A: 오, 비관적이 되지는 말자고. 몇 가지 결정은 내렸니? 어떤 시장에 들어가고 싶어?

B: 나는 재교육을 받고 처음부터 시작하고 싶어.

Scene 9 (45)

Film dialogue and vocabulary   p. 72~73

W: 그린 씨, 왔군! 마침내 만나게 돼서 정말 반갑소.

O: 혼자인가요?

W: 그렇소. 그게 놀라운가? 내가 위험에 처한 거요?

O: 그야 모르죠.

W: 내 개인적인 안전은 아무 의미 없소. 중요한 건 갚아줘야 할 해묵은 원한이지. 그러니 날 위해 가져온 서류를 빨리 받고 싶군!

tell the truth

O: 문제가 좀 생겨서 서류를 가져오려면 시간이 더 필요해요! 하루나 이틀 정도요···

W: 정말 유감스럽군. 올리브! 어쩔 수 없이 당신을 벌줘야겠소··· 당신이 사랑하는 사람들에게 고통을 줘야지! 당신 엄마부터!

O: 제발요! 부탁이에요!

`lie`

O: 제 파트너가 가져올 거예요… 돈부터 확인한 다음에요!

W: 그래, 내가 거금을 주겠다고 약속했었지. 별로 감동한 것 같지 않은데! 단지 시간을 끌려는 것 같은 느낌이 드는 건 왜일까? 서류를 안 가지고 왔다는 뜻인가?

O: 없어요, 하지만…

W: 정말 실망이군! 이런 식으로 날 실망시킬 줄은 몰랐는데!

O: 성급한 결정을 할 필요는 없잖아요!

W: 걱정 마시오! 난 아무도 안 죽일 거니까. 난 머리와는 달라. 적어도 그 자식보다 도덕적으로 우월하다고 생각하고 싶군!

M: 마틴 윌리스 그리고 그린 씨 – 둘이 짠 거군! 미안하지만 놀랍지도 않아!

Communication situations   p. 76~77

Ann: 모두들 안녕하세요, 그리고 와 주셔서 감사합니다. 오늘 의제는 5개로 이루어져 있습니다; 하지만, 먼저 논의해야 할 문제가 있습니다. 존, 이제 당신 차례예요.

Dialogue 1

John: 고맙습니다. 단도직입적으로 말씀을 드리면, 주 공급업체와 관련된 문제가 있습니다.

Ann: 죄송하지만 그 문제는 지난 달에 다루지 않았나요?

John: 실제로 논의는 했지만 결론에는 도달하지 못했죠.

Ann: 그렇군요. 그 문제는 한 번 더 다루기로 해요.

John: 그쪽의 새로운 가격 리스트로 인해 우리가 악영향을 받아서 우리는 협력 관계를 종료시키고자 합니다.

Ann: 그렇다면 왜 이 문제를 다시 언급하고 있는 거죠?

John: 나머지 의제들이 정말로 따분한 것이라서요.

Ann: 당신 생각만큼 재미있지는 않군요.

John: 그들은 수년간 우리의 비즈니스 파트너였으니까요.

Ann: 그건 일리가 있어요. 하룻밤 사이에 비즈니스 관계를 끊으면 우리에게 도움이 되지 않을 수도 있으니까요. 어떻게 하면 좋을까요?

John: 다시 협상 테이블에 앉아서 진상을 파악해 보는 것이 어떨까요?

Ann: 솔직히 말하면 도움이 될 것 같지는 않지만, 당신이 원한다면 그렇게 하세요.

Dialogue 2

John: 고맙습니다. 모두들 잘 아시다시피, 노조와 경영진 간에 마찰이 있어요.

Ann: 네, 그래요. 우리는 해고를 하느냐 보수를 낮추느냐에 관한 딜레마에 빠져 있죠.

John: 문제를 다른 방식으로 해결하는 것은 어떨까요?

Ann: 흥미롭군요. 계속 해 보세요.

John: 우리가 해고될 사람들에게 새로운 일자리를 찾아 주는 거죠.

Ann: 우리가 노동 시장에 개입하는 것이 무슨 의미가 있는지 잘 모르겠군요.

John: 제가 그에 관한 해결의 실마리를 알려 드릴게요.

Ann: 그래요.

John: 노조와 협력하면 파업의 가능성이 줄어들게 되죠.

Ann: 설득력이 있는 주장이라는 점은 인정해야겠군요. 조만간 파업이 한 번 더 발생할 수도 있으니까요.

Scene 10 (46)

Film dialogue and vocabulary p. 80~81

그래, 내 손가락들이 부러지면서 일이 복잡해졌어. 손가락 관절 두 개가 완전히 으깨졌었거든…

그래, 더럽게도 아팠지! 그래, 핀 같은 걸 두 개 삽입했는데… 뼈마디를 지탱하려고 손에 철사 조각을 넣은 거지, 안 그러면…

그래, 맞아. 그래서 새 스마트폰으로 바꾸고 손가락으로 메뉴를 조작하는데… 더럽게 끔찍했어! 손에 불 난 줄 알았어! 못 견디겠더라니까. 그래서 내 월급 절반이나 나가는 이 휴대폰 정말 쓸데없다니까!

M: 올리브, 총을 버리는 게 현명할 거야. 그럼 목숨은 부지할 수 있겠지. 장담은 못 하지만.

W: 날 알아보겠나?

M: 알아보겠냐고? 이 한심한 양아치 녀석! 길에서 널 때려준 이후로 널 지켜보고 있었어. 수년간 날 감시했겠지만, 나도 널 감시하고 있었지.

W: 네 말 안 믿어!

M: 그래? 그럼 내가 왜 여기 있겠어? 네가 항상 믿었던 누군가가 그동안 내 돈을 받아왔기 때문일까? 충분히 가능하지, 안 그래? 사실, 진작에 널 끝장냈어야 했는데… 네가 크는 걸 지켜보는 게 너무 재미있더라고.

Communication situations p. 84~85

A: 그래서, 일을 그만두었단 말이지. 매우 대담한 행보로군. 구직 활동은 시작했어? 네게 제안할 일이 있어서 묻는 거야.

Dialogue 1

B: 고마워 친구, 하지만 관심은 없어. 나는 전자상거래 쪽에 진출할 것이거든.

A: 오, 그래? 장족의 발전이군. 언제 시작할 거니?

B: 대략 한 달 후에.

A: 잘 됐구나! 무엇을 취급할 거니?

B: 나는 온라인 환전소를 운영할 거야.

A: 흥미로운걸. 어떻게 운영되지?

B: 간단해. 내 계좌에 돈을 넣으면 네가 원하는 만큼 내가 네 계좌로 환전을 해 주는 거야.
A: 꽤 명확한데. 하지만 돈을 어디서 끌어올 건데?
B: 그것이 사업의 메인 파트이지. 전 세계 온라인 시장에 들어가 봐.
A: 맙소사. 마치 물을 만난 물고기 같구나. 널 위해 행운을 빌게!

Dialogue 2

B: 그게 뭔데? 네 제안을 고려해 볼 수 있으면 좋겠다.
A: 알다시피 나는 온라인 사업을 할까 생각 중이야. 유일한 문제는 내가 현금에 익숙해서 온라인 거래를 신뢰하지 않는다는 점이지.
B: 온라인 사업은 좋은 아이디어지. 내가 어떤 일을 담당하게 되니?
A: 네가 사업의 자금 흐름과 전체적인 재무 분야를 맡아 줬으면 좋겠어.
B: 네게 도움이 될 수 있다면 기쁘겠어.
A: 성사됐군! 그럼 이제 세부적인 사항에 대해…

Dialogue 3

B: 현금이 최고지. 나도 알아. 하지만…
A: 무슨 말이니?
B: 현금과 인터넷은 같이 갈 수 없어.
A: 지켜만 보라고! 나는 전자상거래의 새로운 모델을 개발하는데 있어서 선구자가 될 테니까.
B: 여기서 불길한 예언을 하고 싶지는 않지만 온라인 결제 시스템이 없다면 네 사업은 실패하고 말 거야.
A: 정말이야, 믿어 봐! 그것이 핵심이라고! 복잡한 "온라인 결재"는 없고 현금만 가능한 거지. 그러면 같이 할래, 아니면 빠질래?
B: 정신 차려! 잘 될 리가 없어! 이 분야는 내가 잘 알거든.
A: 확실히 이 문제에 대해서는 우리 의견이 일치할 것 같지가 않군. 음, 경기를 지켜보자고, 곧 시작될 테니.

Scene 11 (47)

Film dialogue and vocabulary   p. 88~89

M: 사실, 오늘날의 널 만든 데는 내 공로도 있다고 봐.
W: 날 만든 공로? 이 과대망상 멍청이!
W: 넌 내 인생을 망쳤어! 그녀의 인생도! 나에게서 베아트리스를 뺏지 않았다면…!
M: 다시는 그 이름 입에 올리지 매! 듣기만 해도 머리 아파! 아내와는 아무 상관 없다는 걸 너도 알잖아! 인정해! 지난 29년 동안 널 움직이게 한 건 잃어버린 사랑에 대한 미련이 아니야. 나한테 복수하고 싶었던 거지. 하지만 절대 못 할 거야! 그래서 기분이 어떤가? 악몽이 현실이 됐나? 올리브, 나한테 폴더 주고 이 한심한 일을 마무리하자고.

O: 나한테 없어요!

M: 없다고? 이 자가 가졌나?

O: 아뇨, 폴더가 없어졌어요.

M: 없어져? 어디에 있는지 모른다는 건가?

D: 나한테 있어요!

M: 이거 정말… 왜! 내가 또 다른 애송이를 남자로 만든 건가?

D: 이게 어떻게 끝날지는 내가 말해주지! 일단, 당신의 소중한 폴더 여기 있어! (…)

M: 이 느낌 낯설지가 않아… 네가 내 앞에서 한심하게 진흙탕을 기어 다니는 느낌…

M: 하지만 이번엔…

Communication situations p. 92~94

David: 저 소리는 뭐지? 엄마예요? 괜찮으세요?

Dialogue 1

Jessica: 아니. 이 설명서를 읽는 게 이번이 세 번째란다.

David: 그래요. 천천히 하세요. 어떤 설명서인데요?

Jessica: 이 믹서기에 관한 설명서야.

David: 그렇군요. 무슨 문제인가요?

Jessica: 여기를 봐. "먼저 용기를 전원이 들어오는 본체에 꽂아야 합니다."라고 되어 있어.

David: 거기에서 이해가 안 되는 부분이 무엇이죠?

Jessica: 어떤 용기를 말하는 거지? 상자에는 두 개가 있는데.

David: 둘 다 되죠. 용기를 제자리에 꼽지 않은 채 믹서기 전원을 키시면 안 돼요, 그게 다예요.

Dialogue 2

Jessica: 내가 기술에 대해 전혀 모르는 거니, 아니면 날씨 때문이니?

David: 둘 다 아닌 것 같은데요. 무슨 문제인가요?

Jessica: 이 어플리케이션에 계정을 등록하려고 하는데 되지가 않는구나.

David: 엄마, "로그인" 버튼은 그만 클릭하세요, "등록"이나 "계정 만들기"를 하셔야 해요.

Jessica: 맞아… 이미 가지고 있는 계정으로 로그인을 하는 거지! 내가 어리석었구나!

David: 좋아요. 그 다음 단계가 무엇인지 볼게요. 개인 정보와 이메일을 요구하는군요.

Jessica: 그건 쉽구나. 보렴.

David: 멈추세요! 뭐 하시는 거예요? 진짜 이름하고 생년월일은 알려 주시 마세요!

Jessica: 왜 안 되는데?

David: 인터넷이니까요! 누군가가 엄마의 정보를 악용할 수도 있어요. 주의하셔야 한다고요.

Dialogue 3

Jessica: 컴퓨터가 나를 좋아하지 않는구나.

David: 무슨 말씀이세요? 무엇이 문제죠? 제가 도와 드릴까요?

Jessica: 5분 간격으로 작동이 멈춰.

David: 나쁘게 들리네요. 보증 기간 이내인가요?

Jessica: 잘 모르겠다. 그런 것들은 버렸는데.

David: 보증서를요? 진담이세요? 어이가 없군요.

Dialogue 4

Jessica: 블로그를 시작해 보고 싶은데 절차가 이해되지 않는구나.

David: 블로그요? 좋아요. 먼저, 공개 블로깅 플랫폼을 호스팅하는 서버를 찾으셔야 해요.

Jessica: 그건 모두 알고 있어. 기술적인 측면에서 헤매고 있는 거야.

David: 음, 그러면 패널에 로그인하셔서 블로깅 플랫폼을 설치하셔야 해요. "홈페이지 빌더" 아래에 있을 거예요.

Jessica: 그래. 이제 시작해 볼게. 또 도움이 필요하면 너를 찾으마.

Scene 12 (48)

Film dialogue and vocabulary   p. 96~97

D: 젠장! 과다출혈로 죽겠어요! 병원에 데려다줄게요!

O: 병원에는 못 가요! 경찰에 신고할 거예요! 주소를 알려줄게요.

D: 무슨 주소요? 이러다가 죽어요! 의사가 필요해요!

O: 브룩스가… 의사예요. 일종의 의사죠… 젠장, 아파요! 돈… 돈요!

D: 이 상황에 돈 생각이 나요?

O: 그게 아니라… 브룩스 줘야 해요. 그 돌팔이가… 비싸거든요!

M: 머리일세. 올리브 일 때문에 전화했네.

M: 그래, 내가 처리할 수 있다고 한 건 아는데, 그런데 그게… 그래, 회수했어. 그런데 일부 자료가 사라졌는데… 그게… 우리 일과 관련된 거야. 당신 사업엔 지장 없게 하겠다고 약속은 했지만 당신 부하가 실패하는 바람에 내가 직접 나선 거잖아, 안 그래? 알았어. 당신 사무실에서, 내일 정오에. 그런데 일단 손을 좀 써줘야겠어. 총싸움이 있었어. 거기에 있던 사람 중에 생존자들이 있을지도 몰라. 그들이 나에 대해 알아. 그러니까… 부하들을 보내서 그들의 입을 막아줄 수 있겠나? 보상은 해주지, 게다가! 약속해!

Communication situations   p. 100~101

A: 안녕하세요, 신사 숙녀 여러분, 와 주셔서 고마워요. 안건에서 알 수 있듯이 우리는 작년도 판매 실적에 대해 이야기할 거예요.

Dialogue 1

B: 그러면 시작합시다.

A: 저희는 프레젠테이션을 네 부분으로 나누었어요.

B: 앞의 세 부분은 해외에서의 성장에 관한 원 데이터를 설명합니다.

A: 네 번째이자 마지막 부분은 질문을 받기 위한 것이고요.

B: 그렇기는 하지만, 의문이 있는 경우에는 언제라도 진행을 중단시켜 주십시오.

A: 서론은 이것이 끝입니다. 자, 첫 번째 슬라이드를 보시죠.

Dialogue 2

A: 우리의 시장 점유율을 보여 드리는 것으로 시작하고 싶군요.

B: 그리고 난 다음에는 우리의 위치에 영향을 미치는 요인들과 관련된 두 번째 파트로 넘어갈 거예요.

A: 내부적인 요인과 외부적인 요인 모두에 초점을 맞추고자 합니다.

B: 세 번째 파트로 넘어가서는 제기된 문제에 대해 진단을 내리고 대략적인 해결 방안을 제시할 것입니다. 또한 앞으로의 발전을 위한 몇 가지 제안 사항도 제시할 것이고요.

A: 그리고 마지막에는 프레젠테이션의 주요 논점들을 모두 간략히 되돌아 볼 것입니다.

B: 신사 숙녀 여러분, 시작하겠습니다. 프레젠테이션에 대해 말씀을 드리면, 짧을 수록 더 좋은 것이죠.

Dialogue 3

B: 먼저 작년에 이루어진 예측에 대해 이야기를 할 것입니다.

A: 아시다시피 상당히 낙관적이었잖아요.

B: 나중에 판명된 것처럼 너무 앞서 갔어요. 이후에 다시 제자리로 돌아왔죠.

A: 두 번째 슬라이드는 백분율로 이루어진 막대그래프를 나타냅니다.

B: 우리와 경쟁사들을 비교해 주죠.

A: 이에 대해서는 나중에 보다 상세히 살펴볼 것이므로 도표를 잘 기억해 두십시오. 하지만 지금으로서는…

memo

Olive Green

memo

Olive Green

memo

Olive Green

memo

Olive Green